# ESSENTIAL PARENTING™

## Revitalizing and Remoralizing
## The Family in the 21st Century

*To a great guy!*

*Domenick J Maglio*

## By Domenick J. Maglio, Ph.D.
## With Julie Maglio, BA

Wider Horizons Press
4060 Castle Avenue
Spring Hill, Florida 34609

I

ESSENTIAL PARENTING™
REVITALIZING AND REMORALIZING PARENTING IN THE
21ST CENTURY
Is dedicated to our four children who raised us well,
our Wider Horizons School students and parents, clients and their
families who have taught us many of the concepts contained in this
book,
and to all high functioning families who have succeeded
in one of the most, if not the most, important tasks
in a person's life-raising children
This legacy does not only reach the immediate
family, but the succeeding four generations that follow.
Sociologists call this child-rearing impact on the five generations
whether good or bad, the "Five Generational Rule".
The Maglios dedicate this book
to the many generations to follow.

# ABOUT THE AUTHORS:

Dr. and Mrs. Maglio have seventy combined years in the education/psychology area. Their experiences have included: teaching and directing in public and private schools, including preschool, elementary, junior high, senior high and the university level. They have also developed nuclear schools in the jungle of Peru while in the Peace Corps. Dr. Maglio's professional career has ranged from counselor at Wiltwyck School for Boys, school psychologist, nine years at the university level in psychological/educational departments, clinical-psychologist in a Florida state prison, Certified Reality Therapist, ten years directing a domestic violence counseling program, psychotherapist for over twenty five years as a licensed mental health counselor, director for the Open Door for Mental Health Program, staff psychologist at the Eckerd Foundation as well as serving on the Board of Directors of the National Independent Private School Association. In addition since 1983, Dr. and Mrs. Maglio have owned and directed Wider Horizons School, a private k-12 college preparatory school. The Maglio family was fortunate to have Mrs. Maglio be a stay-at-home mother for the first ten years of the children's lives.

Dr. and Mrs. Maglio began their college careers at SUNY at New Paltz, a bastion of liberal education during the beginning of the anti-establishment "hippie" movement of the 1960s. Their Peace Corps experience as well as Dr. Maglio's M.A. degree from the University of Connecticut and doctoral degree from Union Insititue testifies to the depth of their exposure to core liberal and socialistic ideals. As with most idealistic youth, the Maglios charged out to change the world only to find out the world was far different from the "ivory tower" the professors led them to believe. The Maglios learned from colleagues in the field but more importantly, from their own children, students and clients. It was through their first hand experience with real situations that the principles and tenets of <u>Essential Parenting</u>™ began to emerge. The Maglio's have had many professional successes, but are most proud of having raised four highly successful, independent-thinking children to adulthood.

# TABLE OF CONTENTS

## ACKNOWLEDGEMENTS

We would like to thank the following: Mr. Jack Trimpey, Dr. and Mrs. Lester Glick, Mr. Nicholas Morana, Mr. Dan Kane, Dr. Gerry Schneider, Mr. Alan Civillo, Mr. Alan Cavanaugh, and our four children who helped and encouraged the writing of this book. We appreciated their suggestions and ideas which clarified some of the concepts presented.

We thank our editor, Mr. James Taylor, for his organizational and conceptual expertise and layout editor, Mr. Russ Goode, for his artistic work in putting the book together.

We thank Mrs. Rosemarie Geraci for all her secretarial help, Mrs. Pat Dangle for her creative effort and the staff at Wider Horizons School for their everyday implementing of Essential Parenting™ .

# ESSENTIAL PARENTING™:
## REVITALIZING AND RE-MORALIZING THE FAMILY
## IN THE 21ST CENTURY

## Introduction

*"For the hand that rocks the cradle is the hand that rules the world." William Ross Wallace*

In the past thirty-five years of professional life Dr. and Mrs. Maglio have seen American parents become more and more confused as to their role and less and less knowledgeable of what comprises good child-rearing practices. In essence, they have seen a disconnect between modern day parenting and child-rearing practices which have worked over the ages. They have seen the middle, upper class, "me generation" of the 1960s become the child-rearing standard bearers for all social classes in our society. Children are showered with material things while becoming paupers for parent involvement, especially in transmitting culturally approved habits, values, and knowledge. This "affluenza", or over-abundance of material things, is infecting the spirit and soul of the child.

Parents appear confused by their child's ungrateful entitlement mentality and frequently hostile actions. Even though the child demands, and for the most part gets, everything she wants, today's child rarely expresses genuine appreciation and has a constant pout plastered on her face. Yet modern parents appear to be blind to their children and act as if their children are healthy and happy even though they are required to take psychotropic drugs to function in school and at home. It appears that modern parents are unwilling to face and deal with the reality of their children's behavior, but grandparents, childless persons, and professionals

1

frequently perceive the sadness, self-centeredness, and anger of many of today's children. Confused modern parents may be in a paralyzed state, but this acknowledgement of bratty behavior, or "brat lash", is occurring on many levels of society

Dr. and Mrs. Maglio believe the modern-confused parents' refusal to face the reality of the child's behavior is a consequence of a lack of courage. Many modern parents are too fearful to critically examine the behavior of their child, their career obsession, and the confusing messages and rationalizations they receive from today's "psychobabble" experts. To raise a child and socialize him to become a functioning adult takes courage, a real dedicated commitment of energy, focused priorities, thought, and a substantial amount of time to teach the sense which in the past was called "common sense" but is today rather uncommon. This time commitment to parenting cannot be negotiated. "Quality time", even sprinkled with high doses of positive reinforcement of mediocre behavior called "false esteem", cannot compensate for time lost. Quantity Time is necessary for monitoring, seizing, and creating the opportunities for training in loving, obedience, independence, critical thinking, creativity, facing reality, pain, conscience development, empathy, will power, and developing common sense.

Essential Parenting™ makes it obvious to the reader that the prevalent cultural relativist/permissive/materialistic child rearing approach overwhelmingly represented in the mass media is not only ineffective but, much worse, destructive to the healthy development of the child and society as a whole. The proponents of the permissive/materialistic approach have coerced the average American parent, through fear of traumatizing their child, to abandon their instincts and methods of their forefathers and replace them with counterproductive, conflicting, and often confusing concepts. Not surprisingly, many parents have come to dread and even hate their role as parents. The medical and psychological establishment has indoctrinated the confused parent to believe that spanking a toddler will cause the child to become a psychologically abusive adult. However, throughout history and throughout most of the rest of the world, this method of punishing misbehaving children has not led to masses of abusive adults.

Ironically the medical/ psychological establishment has little motivation for the prevention of disorders and great motivation for creating and labeling mental health disorders. Their position is stated by Steve. E. Hymann, M.D., The Director of the National Institute of Mental Health in Psychology Today, May-June 2000: "About 13.7 million children under age 18 about 1 in 5 has a diagnosable mental disorder, six million children have a serious emotional disturbance."

In other words, the medical/psychological establishment has the audacity to state, after propagandizing our American parents to modern medical/ psychological practices over the past forty years, that approximately twenty percent of our children have mental disorders. This 20% figure is of epidemic proportions. An Associated Press report from June 6, 2000 entitled "Study: More Kids Troubled" cites research that finds the diagnosis of emotional and learning disabilities in children has more than doubled from 1979 to 1996. Either our current population of children is defective or environmental factors are causing mental problems or the standards of acceptable behavior are unclear, conflicted, and not based on principles that result in developing healthy children. An objective examination of the inconsistent and faddish child-rearing notions that exist in today's current culture forces one to conclude that the last explanation is the most powerful, plausible and profound. The medical/psychological establishment needs to take responsibility for this wide spread wake of emotionally and socially maladaptive children.

These confused parents, even though they are faithfully following the psychological experts, view themselves as ineffectual failures as parents and their children as people the parents dislike. These confused parents are genuine in their desire to be good parents, attempting to disguise their frustration by pretending to be calm while they are very much in conflict. The lack of positive results is handled by appeasing and attempting to ignore their child's misbehavior. Many modern-confused parents have exhausted all the strategies of the permissive/materialistic approach and feel defenseless against insensitive brats they realize they had the major responsibility of creating.

This book is intended to bring modern parents out of their confusion and frustration into awareness of the lost art of child rearing. The Maglios have used the knowledge of <u>Essential Parenting</u> ™ that they have acquired to improve the quality of life of thousands of individuals and families. This book brings <u>Essential Parenting</u>™ tenets to the reader and helps to implement those tenets in daily life. The parents equipped with these tenets will once again reign as the head of the family, while the child will once again be effectively protected, nurtured, and trained as a child should be to meet his unique needs.

Returning a child to his rightful place as the child and the parent to the top of the family organizational chart will bring a sigh of relief to anyone who believes in a civilized society. This society would be:

- A society where morals, manners, community interest, and responsible choices are prevalent, where thinking and behavior, respect and self-discipline, cooperation, and courage are practiced.
- A society where parents can be proud of their children and the children can be proud of their parents.
- A society that helps children learn the correct behavior rather than documenting and labeling a child as a failure before she has hardly begun her life.
- A society where parents take the responsibility for disciplining and training their child to become an exemplary member of the community.

4

Essential Parenting™, (EP) efficiently focuses parental time and energy and creates a strong family and community, which are necessary for the survival of the family and the preservation of traditional values from cultural relativists. The cultural relativists are people diametrically opposed to the traditional universal\ Judaic-Christian values, believing instead that everything is dependent on the particular situation. This belief in situational ethics denies that absolute values can or should exist. In order to win their argument the cultural relativists have been undermining all traditional values and dumbing down our standards and expectations into mediocrity. Proponents of cultural relativism are waging cultural civil war against traditional family values. EP parents will have the knowledge and tools necessary to counter the relentless assault on traditional values. EP parents can then protect their children from accepting perversion and mediocrity as normal.

Ironically as the many modern-confused citizens have become more tolerant of social deviancy, they have become more intolerant of people living a traditional life style. Disciplining one's child to develop socially acceptable behavioral patterns is considered a "mean" approach while ignoring or appeasing a child's inappropriate behavior is considered a "proper" approach. Discipline has historically been a sign of the parent's love for their children. Today many traditional parents are looking over their shoulders when disciplining their children for fear of appearing abusive to other citizens. Yet individuals with social deviancy or criminal backgrounds are hired to work intimately with children in positions such as teachers, counselors, coaches, and scout leaders. In our mass media traditional values are unmercifully and systematically ridiculed while deviancy is celebrated.

The solution to the disintegration of our values, standards and expectations is not universal infant and preschool government programs which only will continue to allow the cultural relativists to brainwash our children with their materialistic and socialistic agenda. The solution to the root of our nation's problems is not a political reorganization following the lines of socialism, fascism, or one world government headed by international corporations. The solution is not mass medicating the current generation of children. The solution is a strong, viable family headed by two parents with moral strength and integrity. It is a return to the Judeo-Christian ethic and the development of individual character with values passed from one generation to the next by the family. It is a strong nation based on right and wrong role modeling taught by everyone, but primarily by the parents. Perversion is shunned not embraced because of the negative impact on the impressionable child and, ultimately, on society as a whole.

Essential Parenting™ resuscitates the cultural child-rearing knowledge, values, standards, and expectations that are the great legacy of our forefathers. EP uses a sequential process that is built on the foundation of love proceeding from simple behaviors to complex internal morals, values, and beliefs that have been tested through time. This love is traditionally expressed maternally through nurturing and paternally through Purposeful Discipline. This is not a weakened and corrupted form of discipline that is nothing more than a disguise for appeasement of the child. Instead, it is a Purposeful Discipline that returns a healthy dose of fear of the parents to the child, which is essential for respect. It establishes clear and precise parameters as well as sets limits and expectations that maximize the child's internalizing the lessons of the external discipline.

This Purposeful Discipline may appear to be toxic medicine in the present, confused culture contaminated by cultural relativism, yet nothing could be further from the truth. This time-tested medicine might be, in the beginning a bitter pill to swallow for the permissive/materialistic parent, but as the child's behavior becomes more appropriate, this medicine becomes seen as God sent. This Purposeful Discipline is neither toxic nor abusive, but a true form of love that is referenced and acknowledged throughout the Bible. Only through an initial environment of love and meeting basic needs can a parent proceed to the more abstract form of Purposeful Discipline, preparing children through Essential Parenting™ to become fully functioning adults with morals, values, and critical thinking ability. These new adults will then have beliefs that will sustain their own development of a family and become contributing members of society. Essential Parenting™ empowers parents to better deal with their children. This creates a healthier environment for both parents and children.

Essential Parenting™ has ten guiding and supporting principles which are essential in understanding the rationale of this program. Dr. and Mrs. Maglio arrived at these guiding principles while searching for the truth in their work with families and children over a thirty-five year period. "The healthy families who have passed through our lives have taught us these guiding principles which are essential for creating healthy children."

# GUIDING PRINCIPLES

**TRADITIONAL FAMILY IS THE BASIC UNIT OF SOCIETY** Any attempt to replace the family with a government unit has historically failed, preceding the decline and eventual collapse of the society.

**PURPOSEFUL DISCIPLINE** is the intentional teaching or training a more accomplished person gives to another to help on their journey through life. It is a demonstration of love.

**QUANTITY TIME** is the length of time parents spend with their child. The greater the quantity of time the more the parents have the opportunity to share experiences and exploit the moment in order to maximize the overall positive <u>Essential Parenting</u>™ impact on the child.

**ASAN** means <u>Essential Parenting</u>™ should start <u>As Soon As Needed.</u> At the first sign of inappropriate behavior the parent initiates training.

**POISE** <u>Parental Observation-Indication-Strategization-Evaluation</u> is an on-going process by which parents gain assurance and poise in their interactions with the child. Through observing the child's behavioral reactions, the parents can individualize consequences for their child.

**LEAST RESTRICTIVE YET EFFECTIVE CONSEQUENCE** means <u>Essential Parenting</u>™ uses the minimal consequence that gets the desired result.

**MODERATE AND BALANCED CONSEQUENCES** are reasonable and measured responses to an individual behavior that attempts to remain in the middle of the continuum from ignoring to abuse.

**JUST RIGHT MORAL CONSEQUENCE** is an individualized approach in judiciously choosing the morally correct and meaningful consequences for a specific child's actions or expressed thoughts in a particular situation.

**INCREMENTAL AUTONOMY THROUGH EARNING PRIVILEGES** As the child demonstrates constructive behavior he is gradually given greater privileges until he becomes independent.

**DO NOT LABEL, INSTEAD TEACH COMPENSATION**
Compensation is a process by which a person who is unable to resolve a problem using a common approach employs effort, ingenuity and perseverance to overcome the obstacle rather than surrender to the problem. Labeling is a counter productive process that gives the child a built-in rationalization for accepting his own limitations and creating a victimized, "can't do" attitude.

These ten principles are the foundation for development of the rationale of Essential Parenting™. Dr. and Mrs. Maglio developed these guiding principles through working with children and their families in many settings over many years. The Maglios learned through hands-on working in the trenches of educational and psychological settings what truly works in the long run for students and clients. It is from the thirty-five years of experience that they have pieced together Effective Parenting™.

The Maglios were surprised and impressed that modern day Essential Parenting™ is firmly rooted in the ancient teachings of the Bible. It was not until the book was substantially formed and quotes were needed to highlight the chapters that the Maglios found that the best quotes which paralleled their work were found

9

in the Bible.  It makes all the sense in the world since the Bible is a composite of the truth that has passed down to us from our ancestors.  This book may not have begun following the teachings of the Bible, but by observing what truly works with parenting, it wound up at the doorstep of Bible teachings.

This book was originally named <u>Basic Training for Parents in the 21<u>st</u> Century</u> .  It was intended to be formatted like a military manual, directing with precise instructions.  It became evident that the practices, which work with children in the real world, were often the direct opposite of what the medical/psychological establishment has been preaching and teaching for the past forty years.  The traditional child rearing values of western culture have been discarded as "old fashioned" relics of the past, to be replaced by new fads and material gimmicks that are not getting the job done in raising healthy children.

Thus, in order to counteract forty years of the cultural relativistic assault  on our ancestor's legacy of child-rearing knowledge, Chapter I: <u>Essential Parenting™ in the Cultural Cross-Tides</u> and Chapter II: <u>Assault on Traditional Values: Erosion of The Family</u> were inserted.  They set the stage and give the reader insight into how our nation has arrived at this junction.  They also clarify how our so-called "expert advise" is contrary to the well being of our children, parents, and the family as a whole.  The chapters following the first two are the nuts and bolts of the book.  Chapters III through VII are more specific in instructing the reader how to teach and train the child to be a highly successful adult.

<u>Essential Parenting™</u> is an answer to enlightening the modern-confused parent to a rational method of integrating the realities of being a parent today with the wisdom passed down from our ancestors to create the best possible environment for the development of the child. Parents who are willing and eager to

give their child the advantage of <u>Essential Parenting</u>™ can successfully overcome the difficulties of life and turn the cultural tide. The hearts and minds of our children are at stake and the parental transfer of strong values as well as mental and spiritual wisdom to the child is the means to insure the supremacy of society's most important social unit: the family. By <u>EP</u> creating a healthy functioning family everyone profits. Parents who effectively lead their children with knowledgeable values and strategies  that work, reduce their stress and are able to appreciate the important child rearing years. The children are more secure with more consistent and relaxed parents. The higher the family and marital satisfaction, the greater the well-being of the family members. <u>EP</u> does take commitment and initial sacrifice but with a significant payoff to parents and children.

<u>Essential Parenting</u>™ will re-moralize child-rearing. Raising a child without a profound sense of right and wrong is a criminal act on the part of a parent. Through specific techniques and training found in this book parents will find a step-by-step approach of developing moral values in a child.  Virtuous behavior, on the part of a child, will insure a legitimate level of success among law abiding citizens while immoral behavior can only provide temporary success until the immoral behavior is exposed to the full view of others.

<u>Essential Parenting</u>™ will produce appreciative, more helpful, compassionate, critically thinking, responsible, and creative children who will possess personal strength enough to take over society and lead us back on the right track to a more balanced world.  In this society, parents would relish the opportunity to be able to pass on their wisdom to the next generation of leaders. Only through this and other effective and efficient child-rearing programs transmitted by the family can we hope to return dignity, integrity and morally based character back to the fabric of our great nation.

BENEFITS OF <u>ESSENTIAL PARENTING</u>™ TO PARENTS:
>Gain or regain control.
>Establish the position as head of the household.
>Become a more confident parent.
>Lose the frustration of being ineffective.
>Eliminate child's tantrums.
>Become the parent instead of the counselor and friend.
>Have more time to nurture, trust, and be proud of your child
>Gain freedom to read, play, and travel with your child


BENEFITS OF <u>ESSENTIAL PARENTING</u>™ TO CHILDREN:
>Having parent in control
>Greater stability
>Will receive discipline desired and needed
>Consistent and effective parenting
>Will become more responsible
>Take more pride in self and work
>Well defined behavioral parameters
>Happier childhood
>More educational success
>Better mental health
>Better functioning family

## Chapter 1

# Essential Parenting™ in Cultural Cross-Tides

*"You give but little when you give of your possessions. It is when you give of yourself that you truly give."* Kahlil Gibron

Children are not born with the necessary behaviors for success in life, nor are they genetically programmed to automatically acquire these behaviors, as they grow older. Thus, effective parenting requires training. Unfortunately, children do not come with an instruction manual for raising them. There are, however, effective traditional practices that have made good parents for generations. These practices do not rely upon government intervention or pharmaceutical medications. Instead, they employ methods that are premised upon the belief that children's behavior ultimately depends upon the quality of parental training.

Essential Parenting™ is a child-rearing book that gleans wisdom from previous generations, critically assesses contemporary culture's values and child rearing scripts, and provides a concise approach to Purposeful Discipline. Parenting requires a real commitment, which cannot be excused because of work schedules, poor health, marital problems, financial difficulties, or other adverse conditions that occur in adult life. This commitment requires a substantial investment in time and energy, but in the long run will produce a loving environment and balanced quality of life for the husband, wife, and children while following the natural flow of our highly involved genetic nature.

Our present American culture has shifted away from the family to self-absorbed hedonism. This has fostered a tendency to extend adolescence while ignoring the natural desire to nurture a family. The self-indulgent trappings of deviant or casual sex, recreational drug use, and abusive behavior invade our daily lives through the blaring megaphone of the mass media. These destructive behaviors have been glorified while traditional values have been routinely derided and ridiculed. This value inversion has exposed our children to a modern culture that is upside down and is contaminating the rest of the world.

The traditional family has always been the sanctuary protecting our children from destructive forces and can continue to play the same role in the present cultural civil war. If we as parents are willing to devote energy and time to create a stable family then we will withstand the assaults by the cultural relativists on our traditional values. Fostering the strength of the family enabled America to become the greatest of nations. Should we blindly continue down the road of the cultural relativist, then our society is destined to crumble in the same manner as all great past civilizations that have turned their backs on the family.

Essential Parenting™ was written to turn the tide. EP gives back the knowledge and the right of parents to be in charge. Parents no longer need to passively endure abuse from their frantic child's struggle to protect himself in an overwhelming, frightening world. In all the animal kingdom, humans have the least developed instincts. In addition to this reality, children are born without any concept of culture. It is therefore imperative that children be trained to learn their culture. This transmission of culture is essential for children to make the quality choices necessary to flourish in a complex world.

Children need to develop life skills necessary for guiding them on the road to independence and eventual adulthood. Parents need to be the leaders in helping children develop these skills. It takes parental courage as well as resolve to battle a child's inherent self-centeredness and primitive urges to meet their immediate desires. Parents need to set the standards, priorities, and expectations- not the child. The parents need to train the child in all cultural aspects: language, manners, social expectations, gender-sibling-child roles, morals and even toilet training. Essential Parenting™ is not always a pleasant endeavor, but it is almost always a true expression of love that promotes well being for everyone involved.

*Hebrews 12:11: No discipline seems pleasant at the time, but painful. Later on, however, it produces a harvest of righteousness and peace for those who have been trained by it."*

For the parent and child to receive these benefits, the Essential Parenting™ trained parent needs to embark on a solid substantial road that is well worn by our ancestors who traveled this way. This road has lost its favor in our present trendy world to the maze of glittering, crisscrossing, fragile roads paved with false notions that abruptly end in confusion and despair. Our nation, at the beginning of the 21st century, is in cultural cross-tides between the traditional Judeo-Christian values of family that made our country great and successful, and a new social order of cultural relativism. To understand how we arrived at this stage one has to look back to the events leading up to this period of cultural upheaval.

# Characteristics of the Agrarian Age

## FAMILY

- extended family
- father is head of family on a daily basis
- families are isolated on farms in small communities

## ECONOMIC

- large families, children are assets on farm
- survival conformity
- satisfied to survive
- simple expectations for a simple life handed down from family member to family member
- family members cohesively interact throughout day

## SOCIAL

- patriarchal rule
- living in the present, interfacing with nature for survival
- children integral part of family and community, have specific expectations

## MORAL

- traditional values part of the fabric of local community, concretely right or wrong
- marriage permanent with interdependent members
- integration demanded of all family members

# Characteristics of Industrial Age

**FAMILY**
- nuclear family
- father's job first priority, mother's role increases in child rearing and discipline
- large families, move to urban centers

**ECONOMIC**
- family members isolated by individual jobs
- culture has many ethnic and regional subcultures,
- attempting to "keep up with Joneses"
- children often exploited, little time for recognition of child
- mother is caretaker, father at work, increasing choices

**SOCIAL**
- autocratic family style
- living in the past, neurotic behavior prevalent
- more rigid expectations coming from multi levels of society

**MORAL**
- traditional values imperfectly practiced, agreement on right and wrong
- divorce rare, depend on each other, family in conflict
- deviants shunned, considered lifestyle choice, "in closet"

# Characteristics of Post Industrial Age

**FAMILY**
- non traditional families: single parent, blended families, grandparents, and homosexual parents
- child often in charge, both mother and father working
- families move to suburban areas

**ECONOMIC**
- small families, children precious prizes and economic liability
- everyone is "the Joneses" - conspicuous consumption
- too many choices
- television and childcare givers are surrogate parents, mothers and fathers work

**SOCIAL**
- mass media homogenized culture
- low expectations, dumbing down standards and over reactions to the rigid expectations of the industrial revolution
- "childocratic" a false democracy really child tyranny
- living for oneself, sociopathic behavior prevalent pampering, entitlement, high levels of child recognition, "false esteem"

**MORAL**
- cultural relativist confused values replacing traditional values
- shattering of family, members isolated and independent
- deviant pride, cause is genetic, "out of closet"

# Characteristics of Essential Parenting™

**FAMILY**
- neo traditional family commitment to family for mental health reasons not economic
- both parents head of the family
- family can function in any setting

**ECONOMIC**
- small families, parents in charge, children pitch in
- sacrifices excessive materialism for time with family
- limits choices for the sake of family's mental health
- living to do God's work, contributing to family and community, family members cohesively interact spending Quantity Time to maximize their love

**SOCIAL**
- strong family culture that censors the media
- definite high expectations towards education and traditional values
- united parental front, parents in charge
- children are integral contributing members of family and are purposefully disciplined

**MORAL**
- return to traditional values by entire family
- consciously create an interdependent family to foster a permanent marriage
- intimacy demanded of family members for the emotional and mental health survival of the family

Once we revisit the past we will be able to focus on how the prevailing social and economic conditions facing modern parents has lead to a worsening of the quality of child-rearing. We will also examine the confusing and counterproductive directives given by mental health "experts" to parents. This will allow us to understand how we have gone astray by abandoning traditional child-rearing practices. It will also permit the parent to break free from the permissive child rearing script that has produced maladjusted children and be able to embrace the tenets of Essential Parenting™.

**Brief Historical Overview**

A brief and broad stroke historical overview of child-rearing is helpful in understanding how and why our nation has arrived at this confusing time in raising a child and what to do to eliminate the confusion. Through a concise review of the Agrarian and Industrial Ages as well as an overview of the current Post-Industrial Age one begins to comprehend how the distinctive economies of these periods have impacted the parental needs, time, and ability to raise their children.

The family in the Agrarian Age was centered on isolated farms in small communities. Children lived not only with parents; but also aunts, uncles, cousins, grandparents, and other members of the extended family. There were clear distinctions in family organization with the father as head of household and elder family members commanding the respect of the children. In the agrarian society, families had many children since they were considered future assets to maintaining the farm. Members of the extended family in the agrarian world had a vested interest and the time necessary to train their children in all aspects of life. They knew close contact with their children would last for the duration of their lives.

Child-rearing began early with set goals and specific timetables for developing responsible family members as soon as possible to assist in the family's fight for survival. Children, as young as possible, were given enormous responsibilities without any need for inducements. The family lived in the present, with their focus on reaping their harvest from the soil. The pace of life was slow, dictated by daily chores and the seasons of the year along with other direct realities of nature. The lifestyle given to children was simple and absolute. Being a conforming family member meant security and acceptance while rebellion often led to ostracism and guilt.

Interactions of the Agrarian Age were confined to family and nearby neighbors. The local community had traditional values that were woven into the social fabric and transmitted from one generation to the next. Marriage was a permanent union based upon practical considerations and interdependence between the members. Family needs superseded personal desires. Individuals defined themselves by their role in the family and community. The family unit lived the virtue of self-reliance. Families felt a duty to care for their sick and elderly. The only social safety net was family and friends, not the welfare state.

The Agrarian Age had the advantage of firmly established intimacy among family members. Children were given precise parameters and well-defined limits. Elderly family members knew they would be cared for and loved through their infirmity. The role of each member in the family and community was unambiguous. In addition, the community provided concrete values of right and wrong. In short, children were brought into a world where there was security and certainty about life.

The Industrial Revolution changed the social landscape by bringing large numbers of disconnected individuals into close proximity. This was a unique opportunity for individuals to acquire sophistication in a multicultural environment. The urban inhabitant could visit museums and learn about art, music, or science. They could also buy tickets to stage performances, musicals, or ball games. The new urban environment provided more interesting interactions with diverse populations, but compromised the ability of the individual to control his destiny. Personal and career options were greatly expanded, but anxiety was also increased as the individual struggled to learn the rules of engagement in this impersonal world. There were opportunities for insights into the cultural aspects of different ethnic populations, but this was accompanied by distrust of other groups and confusion concerning one's position in the family.

The Industrial Age also altered the underpinnings of child-rearing. The extended family became an economic burden instead of an asset, especially after the establishment of child labor laws. Children were mouths to feed- a definite liability. Fathers were off working in industry leaving the mother with the major responsibility of not only child rearing, but also training of the child's working skills and; for most nuclear families, disciplining of the children. The father's job replaced the family farm as the focus of family decisions. The importance of the family was lessened as the hours worked, salary, vacations, and benefits were directly related to the father's work.

In the Industrial Age, a distinction between the family and work developed, isolating the father for the most part, from his children and even his wife. Traditional values were imperfectly practiced and institutions such as marriage began to falter. The accumulation of material wealth began to supplant spiritual goals. The loss of close contact with nature and control of one's time counterbalanced the increased material wealth and social contacts gained. With the breakdown of the extended family and community, there was a corresponding decrease in social intimacy. In the urban environment with so many different cultures and ideas, the culture and traditions of the parents were incompletely transmitted to the children.

The family has moved from urban areas to suburban areas in the Post-Industrial Age. The race to keep up with the Joneses has become moot as all families have become conspicuous consumers. Traditional values have been eroded and replaced with cultural relativism. The institution of marriage has gone from a state of rarely faltering to the majority ending in divorce. The two-parent household of the nuclear family has gradually become more nontraditional with a sharp rise in single parents, blended families, grandparent guardians, and homosexual parents. The family unit has gone from weakening as isolation increased, to many families having been completely shattered. The transmission of culture and tradition has become so incomplete that, in many cases children have an inadequate context to form a belief system.

The mother as anchor of the family is now working outside the family while the father, if the marriage is still together, continues his quest to be the main provider. The workaholic American parents are reaping the dividends of their work effort through gaining unprecedented buying power which is passed on to their children. The modern confused parents are able to increase the range of choices for their children with activities such as karate, gymnastics, dance, and team sports, but are hard pressed when it comes to one of the most important commodities in life: time. The modern parent's career and complimentary social priorities take precedence over the traditional mundane requirements of being there for their children when they come home after school, at meals, at bedtime, or even when they are ill.

Since the burden of entertaining the child becomes too stressful, the children are often sent to camp and other activities to relieve the pressure on the parents. The nanny, babysitter, daycare personnel, or teacher becomes the surrogate parent. The dissolving of distinctive roles of mother and father has lead to much confusion, frustration and at times hostility. The modern child is reacting naturally to feeling disconnected from his parents. In the absence of intimacy with his parents, the modern child lacks the values and beliefs that function as a rudder in guiding behavior. This has lead, in some disturbing cases, to a disconnection between thoughtful reflection, or conscience, and subsequent violent behavior in turbulent times

## The Advantages, Obstacles, and Dilemmas of Modern Parenting

In the present Post-Industrial Age, where material wealth is god, one can readily track how the obsessive commitment to materialism has pressured the parent of this era into a win-lose situation. The Post-Industrial Age parent can win economically by following the mainstream culture, but they lose socially, morally, and as a family by adhering to these cultural directives. Today's families have obtained the highest level of economic affluence in the history of our young nation. Yet they also face time and intimacy obstacles incomprehensible to families as recently as a generation ago.

Mothers are convinced through brainwashing by advertising that they must work, to maintain the high level of consumerism, "essential" in the Post-Industrial Age. The mother and father roles are taken over by a variety of surrogates: childcare workers, government (public) schoolteachers, and the mass media, especially television, that baby-sits the child while spreading the cultural relativist agenda. These caretakers rely almost exclusively on the vague notions of self-concept, equality, and tolerance so that they can feel safe in not imposing traditional values on someone else's child. Obedience, the necessary element in teaching and training other values, is ignored by caregivers to avoid alienating child and parents.

It is safer and easier to ignore the more time consuming and difficult tasks of teaching values such as: responsibility, honesty, duty, respect, integrity, and morality while sticking to the more questionably beneficial values to the soul of the individual. Feeling good about oneself, believing in an equality that does not truly exist in the real world, and having tolerance for all types of behavior do nothing to help the child define himself in a complex world. It requires no conviction for parents and other caretakers to deal with gauging the child's happiness in the moment rather than on what is best in the long run for the child's overall development.

When parents get home from work their guilt level is so elevated that winning the child's favor is more immediately important than carrying out the proper training of the child. Training is indefinitely postponed to win back the child's "love". No responsibility, no limiting, no conscience development is undertaken, because in the short run these would interfere with developing positive rapport with the child. Pampering of the children when the parents are available becomes the customary practice from entertainment to material gifts to positive reinforcement for mediocre behavior to increase the child's self esteem (false esteem). The modern-confused parents are following pages of the permissive psychological script.

Today's children receive over-compensation from the absent parents through a television in every room, computer games, outside activities, designer clothes and nauseating pampering. This over-compensation by our materially prosperous families is a virus attacking them, which has lately been called "affluenza". The child suffering from "affluenza" is not an emotionally or spiritually healthy person and acts out often in a rage at the slightest frustration. The expectation of immediate gratification has become so entrenched that the child is unable to fathom earning privileges or possessions nor is he able to cope effectively with not having what he wants. Prosperous modern-confused parents ignore and deny their child's bratty behavior, but eventually it is recognized and acknowledged by someone.

This recognition and acknowledgment that the child is not reaching the parental vision and the subsequent attempt to remedy it is being called "bratlash". This is a substantially more difficult endeavor since a foundation of Purposeful Discipline is absent. Modern-confused parents, regardless of the number of zeros behind their annual income, are now realizing that they may be winning the financial battle, but this victory is at the expense of developing a child the parent can look at with pride and contentment.

The win-win position of receiving the financial fruits of our labor plus raising a healthy child can be obtained by following Essential Parenting™ in the Post-Industrial Age through the use of focused training energy during the child's sensitive periods. Essential Parenting™ can transform an uncivilized self-centered, insensitive person into a civilized, caring and sensitive individual while the parent's are pursuing their own economic goals. Through Essential Parenting™ parents can have the convenience, wealth, and power of this era with an initial sacrifice of time and energy by relearning the time tested and proven child-rearing methods of their ancestors. Through Essential Parenting™ modern parents win not only economically, but socially and morally as well, by raising a family that is sufficiently healthy to sustain their legacy.

Over the long haul this intense experience of child rearing will provide the dividend of independent children who the parents will not have to economically assist well into their twenties, thirties and even beyond. The Essential Parenting™ child becomes a contributing member of the family in a similar way as did the Agrarian child except the impetus is not the necessity for survival, but the result of conscious, intelligent parent-child choice. The Post-Industrial Age has placed both mother and father outside the

world of their children, but this book will enat[...]
entry and prominence in that world.

## From Authoritarianism to Permissiveness:
## How the Pendulum Has Swung Too Far

The agrarian stage of our history had child rearing as the sole domain of the extended family with the father having daily involvement. In the industrial stage, the family became a nuclear family with the mother having the primary responsibility of child rearing. In the Post-Industrial Age, surrogate parents such as babysitters, nannies, day care workers, teachers, and even the peer drug and sex culture have assumed the responsibility of raising the child. These professional caregivers are educated by "the experts"- medical doctors, psychologists, educators, etc. who appear on television and write books.

These "experts" trace their philosophical notions back to the founding medical doctors, psychologists and educators of the twentieth century such as Sigmund Freud, Alfred Adler, John Dewey, William James, Maria Montessori, and Carl Jung. These founders wrote in response to the social maladies that existed at the time. The Victorian society of the early 1900s had rigid social conventions and restricted personal autonomy. Individuals in this time could defy conventions only to endure enormous guilt or deny personal desires and feel oppressed. The foundation of modern mental health was different variations of the same social remedy: increasing the freedom of the individual while lessening the oppressiveness of the extended family. This theme lead quite naturally to instilling democracy in the family.

Students of these founding fathers have stretched these ideals of democracy and instructed parents to encourage their children as young as possible to have a voice in family decision making. Supposedly by the child having a vote in the family discussion, the

ll have better judgement and more empathy. The problem
this premise is that a democracy only works well with a
owledgeable, responsible, socially aware individual. Children
given the power to make decisions before they internalize
responsible action will often make capricious and self-serving
choices without being able to critically understand or care about
the implications of their decisions. In other words, a child given
decision making power before reaching a sufficiently high
standard of responsibility and critical thinking is like giving a
child the keys to the car before teaching him how to drive.

A child who is led to believe through this artificial democratic
process that his opinion should be given equal weight to an
authority figure's often appears openly defiant. Teachers, bosses,
police officers, college professors, state their expectations and
standards without expecting or entertaining debate. Experts know
what they want and will not suffer arduous negotiations with
children over simple directions. A child who thinks he is entitled
to be on the same footing as an authority figure or any adult will
often appear at best naïve or inappropriate and at worst as
irrational. It is the responsibility of parents to teach children a
balance between conceiving opinions and expressing their views
respectfully to any adult and authority figure.

A child understanding limits as well as the appropriate time and
place to express herself is just as important as expressing her
opinion. Teaching the child that not all situations will be
democratic or fair is an essential lesson for a child to learn in
dealing with real life. Parents often believe they will have the
power to protect rather than prepare their children for life outside
of their direct influence. Unfortunately, the child who does not
respect or adhere to protocol in interactions with authority figures
will find her opinions not given any credence. As a child becomes
more responsible, knowledgeable, and gains greater social
awareness, her opinions and decisions will carry greater influence

and garner acceptance by most reasonable adults.

The ideal of personal autonomy may have led Dr. Benjamin Spock in the 1950's to help shift almost all discussion of child rearing to the side of permissiveness. Permissiveness espouses that the child inherently has the necessary internal mechanism to become a functioning adult with a minimum of guidance from parents. According to this premise, the parent was instructed to rarely intervene and not define expectations. It was presumed that children would naturally reach levels of attainment with little or no structure. In the absence of parameters and boundaries, however, the permissive approach has fostered children being demanding of parents, throwing tantrums without consequences and without any of the rules and responsible actions required of an adult. In essence, the shift from oppressed childhood to the oppressive child has been completed in the Post-Industrial Age.

Nevertheless, our child rearing "experts" still maintain, the less you direct a child the better. "Children will let you know when they are ready to potty train, children should eat what they want, children will learn to listen when they are ready, children will be children." Thus the less damage you do to your child by not directing him, the better off he will be. Many modern experts who once were proponents of "time-out", "grounding", or taking away privileges as an alternative to spanking have shifted so radically as to condemn even these approaches as unacceptable coercion. "Nurturing" and "trust" are the only tools allowed to be used for disciplining a child for the modern parent.

"Time-in" is a new concept that has incorporated this peculiar logic. It advocates that the parent should give the child more positive caring attention when he misbehaves. Could this be the wrong message? The world does not revolve around a particular child and his parents. These overindulgent parents unwittingly produce a narcissistic child. The parents will not always be there

29

to artificially protect this "nonsensical, unrealistic paradise." Parents through time-in are unknowingly promoting an inappropriate behavior. Maintaining this illusion eventually leaves the child without the necessary behaviors to succeed in a competitive world.

There are experts such as William Glasser and James Dobson who discuss enforcing natural and logical consequences on one end of the spectrum. Then there is Susan Miller who relates that children are raised by their peers and not by their obsolete parents on the other extreme. However, the overwhelming majority of "experts" advocate a non-directive, non-judgmental, parenting style. This book breaks ranks with these "experts" and presents an Essential Parenting™ program with specific parameters, limits, and expectations as the best way to raise a healthy child.

In the Post Industrial Age where family members are scattered and have limited time together, a clear and precise training program will enable parents to maximize their teaching and training impact and thus increase the benefits they receive from correctly trained and reasonable offspring. The following list will illustrate how Essential Parenting™ helps the modern-confused parent break the shackles of the ineffective permissive approach and achieve the outcomes they desire.

**Outcomes of <u>Essential Parenting</u>™ in the Post Industrialized Age:**

> parent head of the household
> children receive specific training
> children learn to value family, home, and school
> children develop self-competence through the work ethic,
> children define and expand their personal goals
> children learn to be responsible for their own choices
> > becoming viable, democratic family members
> children become adults who pass on <u>Essential</u>
> > <u>Parenting</u>™ to their children
> materialism is balanced by spiritualism

The Post-Industrial Age parent who commits to the tenets of <u>Essential Parenting</u>™ will end the paralysis of modern day parenting and place themselves back in their rightful position at the head of the family. <u>Essential Parenting</u>™ initially requires sacrifice, but produces great dividends in the long run. By role modeling traditional values, maintaining high standards and expectations for themselves and their children, limiting choices for children until they earn them, spending Quantity Time together, consciously creating an interdependence among family members, praying together, doing God's work, and contributing to family and community, <u>Essential Parenting</u>™ produces a healthy, happy, functioning family in the Post-Industrial Age. On the other hand, the permissive approach, as seen below, yields gratification in the short term, but the lack of discipline inevitably leads to disappointment down the road.

# ESSENTIAL PARENTING™ BEHAVIORAL MATRIX

| ESSENTIAL PARENTING™ | | MODERN-CONFUSED |
|---|---|---|
| SHORT TERM | pain | happiness |
| LONG TERM | happiness | pain |

Essential Parenting™ takes a real commitment on the part of both parents. Continually observing daily behavior and monitoring the children's chores and schoolwork, especially when the parent has a full time career is extremely tiring and emotionally taxing. Regardless of the energy costs, being in charge of your child's destiny in the long run is incredibly valuable as your child accepts your status as being a concerned and "in charge" parent. This allows the child to know the parameters, limits and expectations of the family, thus exploring safe and calm waters in harmony with his parents. When a child has such a healthy respect for the parent's power that the mere thought of the reaction of the parent will in itself be a deterrent to the child committing the misbehavior, then you have the essential element for effective parenting.

Many contemporary child-rearing approaches, as mentioned above, have a laudable goal of wanting to increase democracy in the family. The problem is that a three-year-old lacks the abilities or experiential knowledge of a seventeen-year-old, which will allow him to make the same quality choice. Only through the process of "gradual autonomy through earning privileges" can parents allow the child a greater voice in her family's decisions. A child has to work her way up in a decision making process. If parents abdicate their decision making responsibilities too early it will be a detriment. Rather than creating a responsible mature adult, the outcome to child, family, and society is producing another demanding, irresponsible, narcissistic child or worse, an addiction prone sociopath.

There is probably no more significant stage in a person's life than that of passing on knowledge and wisdom to provide a springboard for his own children's life. Essential Parenting™ gives parents a blueprint for gaining and retaining control during the formative years of their children's development. Essential Parenting™ also provides, through the POISE process, a judicious method to gradually withdraw decision-making authority as the child demonstrates he is making better choices. Parents will then have the security of knowing that their child will have the necessary skills, and knowledge to be successful on his own flight through life, even in the turbulent winds of this cultural civil war.

The next chapter will illustrate how and why traditional values have been devalued and the resultant erosion of the family. First, it will discuss the emergence of cultural relativism. Then, it will briefly outline the methods by which the cultural relativists have assaulted traditional values and the family while infusing their own ambiguous ideals into the culture. The third consideration will be how the cultural relativist agenda promotes the dissolution of the traditional mother and father roles, while increasingly incorporating government care providers and pharmaceutical drugs in the development of children. Finally, it will assert the necessity of revitalizing the family while denouncing the propaganda of permissive parenting and the socialistic child-rearing theory.

Chapter 2

## Assault on Traditional Values: Erosion of the Family

*"Honor thy mother and thy father."*
*Exodus 20:12*

The Post-Industrial Age culture and the family went through a rapid meltdown from the more traditional 1950s to the radical 1960s. The assault on traditional universal values was accelerated through the emergence of the television and mass media. Those values are being supplanted by modern cultural relativism. This cultural relativism has undermined to a significant extent the last foundations of a generally weakened Post-Industrialized Age family. This devaluation of traditional values and the siege on the family has been occurring in incremental steps over the past four decades. The roles of mother and father have been appreciably eroded and the roles of government and medications in the development of children have mushroomed to an alarming proportion. There is every reason to believe that this trend will continue unless a concerted effort is made to revitalize the family.

34

The hippies', anti-establishment values of the sixties have become barnacles on today's social fabric. With nearly forty years of growth these barnacles are overwhelming and gradually sinking the ship of traditional values that have supported and kept our vibrant nation afloat. The anti-establishment values of the sixties originated as a counter-cultural critique of prevailing culture within colleges. The students behind this movement left college and began professional life with a desire to change society. They gradually rose to greater positions of influence over the next three decades. By the end of the century the anti-establishment renegades of the sixties have established themselves in every walk of life including the White House.

At the beginning of the new millennium in the United States, the family is being systematically de-emphasized by these renegades turned reformers. This has laid the groundwork for a bloodless cultural coup that is replacing our traditional values with cultural relativism. The family and our Judaic-Christian values have been practically sacrificed on the altar of the sacred dollar. Personal freedom has been given such emphasis that personal responsibility is submerged by situational ethics. The art of child-rearing with its inherent values is on the brink of extinction. The traditionalists are isolated with immobilized voices while the cultural relativists are seemingly omnipresent. The cultural relativists are dictating the battle and often appear to be on the verge of total victory. In much the same manner the Soviet Union appeared on the verge of victory before the sudden collapse of the Berlin Wall.

The cultural relativists will not be satisfied with greater tolerance of deviant behavior, but seem bent on eradicating all traditional values and institutions while imposing their beliefs on traditional family members. Should they succeed, the society will become morally impoverished and the democratic barriers to a totalitarian state will have been removed. The cultural relativists espoused the

35

virtues of open-mindedness when they were the counter-culture on the outside. Now they have appropriated the majority of information sources: schools, universities, newspapers, television, and movies. The tone has decidedly changed from embracing diverse opinions to steadfastly not tolerating dissent. The original intent may have been expression of freedom although somewhat self-centered, but the cultural relativists will not stop until they control what people believe. Understanding the methods and the ultimate objectives of cultural relativism outlined here requires placing the movement in an historical context.

## The Emergence of Cultural Relativism

The hostile and oppressive rejection of traditional values erupted on the world stage in the early 1900s with the Bolshevik Revolution and after World War II in China, Korea, Eastern Europe, and later Vietnam. The United States was resistant to Marx's utopian cultural relativist notions with our strong history of individual freedom, viable diversified economy, and a large percentage of ethnic immigrants. These immigrants, since they had an agrarian background, lived traditional values including personal freedom and the family. Thus, the environment was not favorable to a socialist revolution. However, this radical, socialistic agenda did exist in the U.S. incubating quietly and slowly in institutions of higher learning and small pockets of intellectuals in our urban centers. Ideal conditions for the rapid explosion of the anti-establishment culture came together in the 1960s: substantial prosperity after World War II, the advent of television, a large "baby boomer" population which entered college in previously unseen numbers through the "open admissions policy", and a large number of young people who were searching for an identity distinct from their parents.

The natural tendency of teenagers to launch themselves from their families as well as gender, racial, and ethnic differences were

36

fanned by the Marxist leaning cultural relativists in higher education. Students were exposed to socialistic propaganda that undermined the value system of their parents. Passion of conviction was distorted to intolerance, belief in God to ignorance, masculinity to oppression, femininity to weakness, parenthood to a mundane lifestyle, discipline to abuse, and personal integrity to naïvete. Natural differences between the sexes, religions, racial and ethnic differences were presented to the students to demonstrate that the entire social establishment was inherently oppressive, corrupt, and closed to outsiders. Pitting one group against another is a commonly used socialistic strategy to gain power. Women's concerns were antagonistically contrasted with men's concerns, black against white, "haves' against "have nots", and children against parents.

The media, especially with the universal access to television by citizens in the United States in the late 1950s and 1960s, began the clever bombardment of anti-establishment messages through music, advertising, movies, and television situation comedies to ridicule traditional values. In the process the media would also laud the social misfit "hippie" for their juvenile acts of rebellion making free sex, drugs, rock and roll, equality, and tolerance of all behavior their value mantra. The shift from families teaching traditional values to their children to the cultural relativists calling the shots was apparent by the 1960s and 1970s. The choreographed use of sex, violence, music, and video has undermined traditional values and has led to parental loss of the power to raise their own children. These values have been replaced by a socialistic agenda spread by the cultural relativists who have used the most sophisticated Hollywood techniques to manipulate emotions and alter thoughts, values, and beliefs. This process has utilized focus groups, "subtle censorship", "spin doctors", dubious scientific research and reporting to advance socialistic commentary. Consider the chart below which demonstrates the gap between constitutional wisdom and cultural relativism:

# COMPARISON

| Constitutional Wisdom | Socialism | Cultural Relativism |
|---|---|---|
| Freedom to practice religion | Religion outlawed | Religion Ridiculed |
| Right to bear arms | Firearms confiscated | Gun control and bans |
| Private property and contracts essential | Collectivism; all property is public | Tax system used to redistribute wealth |
| Freedom of speech (thought) | Re-education camps brainwashing | Sensitivity training, political correctness |
| Family rights inviolable | Communes; children are wards of the state | Government intervenes on suspicion of abuse |

## Assault on Traditional Values

There is no better method to radically transform a traditional society than to attack the underpinnings of the culture: the family. The family is under siege in this cultural struggle, for that is the bedrock in which all traditional values are embedded. The family is the social unit that inculcates children with values such as the work ethic, obedience, moral beliefs, roles of its members, and the importance of sacrificing and giving to family, community and nation.

Hollywood attacks became blatant in the 1970s with "All in the Family" where traditional values were depicted at best as obsolete and at worst as moronic, while the leftist agenda was demonstrated as uplifting and inspiring. Popular television show, "Murphy Brown", of the 1980s preferred unmarried status as a mother. "Married with Children" and "Roseanne" continued the trend in the 1990s and "Ally McBeal" at the beginning of the century continues the tumbling of common decency, which is escalating the destruction of the virtues of the single most important bastion of values, the family.

Anti-family propaganda is not the sole property of television. It is spread in books, radio, magazines, movies, and the liberal biased education system. The average American child spends approximately three to five hours a day usually self absorbed with television, CDs, radio, computer and video games, with little adult interaction to help the child interpret these messages. As the propaganda is disseminated throughout society, more and more people become dissatisfied with their traditional status. These now dissatisfied individuals are like sheep supporting the movement to alter their own identity and values in order to be accepted by the "intellectual elite". These intellectuals attempt to create a world where their flaws and deviance become acceptable social values rather than change their behavior and emotions to fit in a stable and functioning traditional world.

By breaking down the family, previous family members become socially isolated individuals who can easily fall prey to cultural relativism where everything is acceptable without moral condemnation, critical thought or social and legal consequences. The abnormal becomes legitimized and becomes normal. This is where sex, violence, and corruption are so commonplace that individuals protesting these exploitative vices are seen as reactionaries or worse, as extremists in the defense of their universal values. The Hollywood stars, outstanding athletes and charismatic politicians are often self-centered, hedonistic, sociopathic deviants who become our national heroes and the hard working fathers and mothers are disrespected, ridiculed, or more often ignored for their old fashioned values.

Cultural relativism is rapidly replacing our long held traditional universal values. The media bombards American society with images of precocious children who are smarter and stronger than their confused and conflicted parents. The child is the center of attention and is able to get his way through subtle and not so subtle manipulation becoming in his own mind a child of entitlement. The deviants of the recent past have practically become role models. Expectations and standards have been "dumbed down". Gender differences have been eroded to the point where a group of boys and girls are called "guys" and drugs have become the panacea for behavioral and emotional problems in the name of a new social order based on cultural relativism. This new social order can redistribute the spoils of this siege but does not have the substance to hold together our existing society or create a new viable society. The table below offers a summary contrast between traditional values and modern cultural relativism.

## CULTURAL CIVIL WAR

| Traditional Values | Modern Cultural Relativism |
|---|---|
| Parents head of household | Child believes he is head of household |
| A child is obedient to parents | Child is allowed to manipulate parents |
| Strong work ethic-always do your best | Child believes in entitlement doing only enough to get by |
| Gender roles are distinct | Gender roles are blended (unisex) |
| Commitment to being the best parent they can be | Commitment to indulging child and self with material goods (affluenza) |
| Sanctity of family | Equating of deviant life styles with family |
| To serve God | Money and sex as god |
| Mother as homemaker | Mother as career woman |
| High standards and expectations | Dissolving standards dumbing down to mediocrity |
| Inappropriate behavior receives Just Right Moral Consequences | Inappropriate behavior receives rationalization or weak consequences- moral relativism |
| Problems confronted and solved | Drugs can mask all problems |
| Schools have academic orientation | Government schools have socialistic agenda |
| Set limits | No limits |

## Rationalizations of Cultural Relativism

In modern society with a powerfully established mass media, disgruntled individuals can take a deviant position and sell it to the public. When working mothers began to enter the workforce, the propagandists attempted to deny the negative impact on their children by selling them the concept of "quality time". "Quality time" was the slogan that allowed parents to have less and less time with their children and have less and less guilt. The quality not the "quantity" of time was the way of justifying jobs replacing families as our top priority.

This bogus "quality time" rationalization has been so widely accepted in our modern society it has become almost an uncontested truth. Yet mothers seem to have put aside many other important parental responsibilities such as toilet training (from 18 months to 2 years to 3 or 4 years), listening skills and independence training, in order to spend "quality time" with their child. It is true that it would take very strong discipline and focus for a mother to come home from a career job and begin training her child. It feels so much better and takes less energy to give presents and play with the child than take on a "Quantity Time" job of training.

Studies of fathers in the 1970s noted that the average father spent five minutes a day with his children. This highly publicized dubious study would give solace and personal justification for fathers to be in a position that practically removes him from contact with his children. He could spend "quality time" perhaps by taking his child to Disney World twice a year, buying everything the child desires, acquiescing to the child's every whim, rationalizing to himself that he is an exemplary father who should have no guilt for seeing his son only twice a year. The use of parental material wealth to appease a child is a new form of child rearing neglect attacking today's children called "affluenza".

A parent recently said that he tells his son, when the child complains that he misses his father, "You would not have this nice house and all these toys if I didn't work all the time". The child continues to complain and act out indicating that he does not accept the argument.

My personal experience illustrates the importance of Quantity Time with your child. My son, who was eighteen months old, shunned me when I attempted to pick him up after a week long business trip. His reaction was strong and at eighteen months he did not understand nor care about studies of other fathers spending only five minutes a day with their children. That experience made clear to me intimacy requires a substantial and consistent time investment which cannot be substituted with material comforts.

Mothers and fathers know they need more time- Quantity Time- with their child than the experts assert. Allowing a child to sleep in the parent's bed as late as preschool and at times into adolescence is a direct result of the parent's guilt. Parents prolong the infancy stage- babying the child- late potty training, permitting thumb sucking, baby talk, acting "cute" and not teaching the concept of the word "no" even at the late age of six or seven years.

Instead of teaching the concept "no" parents have been inundated by psychobabble to reinforce their child's positive behavior and ignore their unacceptable behavior. This inappropriate use of positive reinforcement for a "get by" behavior creates a false belief in the child. The child internalizes the fact that his poor effort is sufficient to be accepted by other authority figures. The child's self esteem is a false esteem because the reality of social standards will deflate the child's esteem when he receives an F grade, is rejected by the military, or is unable to get the job of his choice. Thus, we have many unsocialized or undersocialized children with high self-concepts and no idea how limited their thinking and skill levels are.

Eventually these children leave the sheltered and delusional world of their parents and face society in the form of school. Even in the public school world of positive reinforcement and the "dumbing down" of standards, many of these children with inflated self concepts face the slow realization that they do not measure up to others. Yet the media continues to trumpet "quality time", positive reinforcement, unconditional love (a synonym for permissiveness) and alternative lifestyles through celebrity testimonials and pseudo-scientific research. The marketing of the liberal cultural relativistic agenda is outstanding. The only problem is that it does not result in healthy, independent, high functioning children. Old-fashioned parental time consuming discipline does.

The cultural relativists also tried to deny the importance of the two-parent family. They felt that parents had an obligation to pursue personal fulfillment that superceded preserving the marriage. This pursuit could be hampered by the confines of marriage. The battle cry shifted from "keeping the marriage together for the sake of the kids" to splitting up for the sake of the kids. It was reasoned that divorced parents who could more freely pursue their own needs would make better parents. However, divorce has turned out not to be the panacea the divorce proponents thought it would become.

Yet the cultural relativist establishment even has had the audacity to attack the importance of fathers in the family. The last two decades of research on fatherless families has demonstrated a correlation between fatherless families and more frequent arrests, drugs and alcohol, with teenage pregnancy, and problems in school. Yet the cultural relativists claim that the only value for a male in the family is his paycheck. Murphy Brown's self-serving and selfish approach of having a child without a father is an attempt to legitimize or even glorify single parenthood. Who needs a man to raise a child? The answer is obvious- the child does.

Recently a parent announced that she chose to have no father for her child. Her statement has a touch of arrogance and an immense amount of ignorance of the consequences to her child. The role modeling of the father, differing perspectives of life, support and assistance of a father are necessary in raising a healthy child. Of course a father substitute can be utilized, though a large commitment on the part of this person is necessary to have the desired impact. Mothers and fathers from two different subcultures need to bounce their thoughts and ideas off each other to be better parents.

A single parent working full time raising a child is practically an impossible task. When a single parent is raising a child alone they often make the child their buddy-friend and share too much of their personal life with them. The lack of another adult in a single parent family home encourages the child to be a substitute partner for the single parent. This further complicates child training and makes for an emotionally conflicted home. Single parenthood can be a successful way of raising a child, although it is a lot more difficult and practically impossible without the aid of supportive others and gender opposite role models such as grandparents, aunts, uncles and close friends. Some mothers and fathers have been able to raise a child without a husband or wife and deserve incredible credit for their personal sacrifices, but they are the exception rather than the rule.

## Socialist Surrogates with Mental Health Miracle Drugs

As the cultural relativists demean the members of the family, they have subtly or not so subtlety replaced these members of the family with the government. Many of the functions of the family have been taken up by government institutions: health clinics, social welfare, WIC programs, day care and public schools. Public (government) schools no longer stick to the basics of teaching academics. The schools have branched out in every direction to fulfill a socialistic agenda. Public schools have taken over the traditional roles of family: feeding breakfast and lunch, on site health clinics, transmitter of values, sex education, condom dispensers, and homosexual acceptance indoctrination. Most public schools offer daycare from two years old and after school. The traditional curriculum has been debased, lowering academics by "dumbing down" the curriculum to mediocrity.

Psychotherapy, and the latest drug, is offered for every developmental behavior that a child displays. The mental health profession has the audacity to label children less than eighteen years old and as young as three with mental health disorders such as depression and bipolar disorder. Incredible as it seems Ritalin and Clonidine, a blood thinner, are being Off Label prescribed for preschoolers when the FDA warning label states it is not to be used for children younger than six years old. Young children will manifest many immature behaviors that the child will naturally outgrow. It was not long ago that a person had to reach eighteen years of age and be observed in several settings before a professional would feel sufficiently comfortable in making a diagnosis that has such a profound life-time impact on the person.

Drugs, such as Ritalin, Paxil, and Prozac used to alter the symptoms of behavior and emotions, are commonly prescribed without simultaneously using counseling to attempt to alter the behavioral dynamics that underlie the cause of the problem. In fact, our experts are continually pushing a new magic pill to either increase academic production, or to reduce anxiety and pain, or to make people feel good, or cure a major physical problem solely by prescribing a pill. The traditional solution of changing a part of one's lifestyle and getting to the root cause of the problem is rarely even considered.

# Revitalizing the Family

*Children act in the villages as they have learned at home.*
*Swedish Proverb*

The family home is the center from which the child learns about himself and the world. It takes committed, knowledgeable and secure parents, rather than a village, to raise a child. The cultural relativists are systematically attempting to replace the traditional family with an artificial village of "employed social experts" such as social workers, teachers, counselors, physicians, paraprofessionals, resource officers, home visitors and even classmate counselors. None of these artificial village members has the long term involvement, commitment and shared moments of a family and is destined to fail as it has failed time and time again in the past.

This invading socialistic village army is not a viable substitute for the historically tested traditional family unit. Throughout history, in the golden age of Greece, Rome, Mesopotamia and the Incan Empire, the abolishment or de-emphasis of the family precipitated the collapse of the entire society. The family is the basic unit of society. It is the collective energy of the family in society, not the direction of government, that is the backbone of civilization. Essential Parenting™ returns the family to its rightful place with an emphasis on Purposeful Discipline administered by both parents.

Purposeful Discipline is an opportunity and privilege that allows parents, traditionally mothers in the early years, fathers in preteen to adolescent years, to inculcate their values in their children. The mother assists the child in learning about the female subculture while the father does the same with the male subculture. Many if not most, young adults have never had the opportunity to live in a functional family with both positive parental role models.

46

Learning through example has been the historical means of becoming a knowledgeable parent. As the cultural relativists have eroded the underlying principles and values of traditional families, the art of parenting is becoming a lost art. <u>Essential Parenting</u>™ attempts to codify the lost art and knowledge of child rearing which was passed from one generation to the next through family members and community elders. The next chapter will focus both on the importance and the techniques necessary to be a parent in charge.

**Chapter 3**

## Being a Parent in Charge

*How sharper than a serpent's tooth it is, to have a thankless child.*
*William Shakespeare*

Loving a child does not mean allowing a child to do whatever he wants or giving him whatever he desires. This is a prescription for a spoiled, thankless child. This prescription is the permissive materialistic approach to dealing with the child. The cultural relativists have shifted the concept of love to the extreme side of the continuum, while discipline training has taken on the stigma of abuse. To love a child is to take the time and energy to teach ancestrally tested moral values and beliefs which give that child inner strength as well as assist him to become a positive force in life.

*Hebrews 12-6 "...because the Lord disciplines those He loves and He punishes everyone He accepts as a son.*

Parents with the experience of life can pass their wisdom on to their children. The reverse does not happen. A child does not have the ability to understand life before living it.  The mature parents need to be the teachers passing on their accumulated spiritual and cultural knowledge to the immature child.  The child has to be the student absorbing all aspects of the culture.  The family is the best vehicle society has for this transfer to take place.  For a family to function properly parents, not children, need to be in charge.

Most parents in the United States today are not in charge.  The children are in command.  Many of today's parents find themselves unable to challenge their children for the authority they rightly deserve as the adults in the household.  The children have long ago taken over that place and are on the top of the organizational chart.  This is an unfortunate situation for both parents and children.

Parents begin to dislike their children because they do not get the same respect from their children that _they_ gave to _their own_ parents.  Their children realize they are not receiving the necessary guidance and become resentful towards their indecisive parents.  The process can only be reversed when the modern-confused parents realize that they are ineffectual and desire better behavior from their children.  Then parents can make the real commitment necessary to parenting a child.

The following charts outline the differences between a traditional, take charge parent and a modern-confused parent.  Parents realize, through Essential Parenting™, that child rearing requires a lifetime commitment of time and energy in order to train a competent child and eventually a competent adult.  Modern-confused parents bestow on the child the power to make decisions to avoid resentments the child might express when the child reaches adulthood.  The fear of being considered by their child as dictatorial, over-controlling parents and/or the fear of making a traumatic mistake leaves parents immobilized, unable to be in charge of the child.  Essential Parenting™ uses Purposeful

Discipline to implement the techniques and strategies needed to be in charge. The modern-confused parent is so neurotically stuck in not doing something wrong that the responsibility of parenting is abdicated.

## PERCEPTUAL DIFFERENCES

| ESSENTIAL PARENTING™ PARENTING | MODERN-CONFUSED |
|---|---|
| Parents are committed to parenthood | Parents are uncertain of their role |
| Parents have courage to be in charge | Parent's fear forces them into friend and counselor role |
| Parents distinguish between child and parent | Parents believe child is equal |
| Parents are ultimate decision-makers | Parents allow unprepared child to be decision-maker |
| Parents understand child's inability to distinguish difference between fantasy and reality | Parents give child credit for distinguishing between between fantasy and reality |
| Parents inculcate values, beliefs and morals in their child | Parents are frightened to impose their own morals on their child |
| Parents views child as their future legacy | Parents view child as temporary inconvenience |

The modern-confused parents have been given erroneous and conflicting information. They have been lead to believe a child can grow and mature effectively without the guidance, assistance, and training of the parent. It has been drilled into the heads of modern parents that imposing their values on a child is stifling to the child's overall creative mental development. It is the belief of modern psychological experts that children should be given the opportunity to democratically choose their own values, beliefs and morals. In reality, the child is not developmentally ready to make rational decisions on his own with limited perceptual accuracy and limited experience. Values, beliefs and morals are culturally transmitted either by wise and knowledgeable parents or by counter subcultures.

It is the responsibility of the parent to inculcate a strong value system in the child. As the child grows, he can modify and adapt this system in his changing world to better function in the world. To leave a child without beliefs, values and morals is to leave the child rudderless on the rough seas of life. If the child is not well trained by the parents she will be deficient in socially appropriate thinking and behavior. This deficient child will be susceptible to being "brainwashed" by negative peers, the drug culture, religious cults, and the violent and sexually explicit mass media.

The modern-confused parent, however, has been handcuffed by current popular psychobabble. According to our psychological experts, if the modern-confused parent has high expectations and the child does not meet these expectations, a neurotic child will be produced. The experts further assert most children cannot behave well (terrible twos, rebellious teens.) It is presumed that the child will "outgrow" the behavioral problems. When the problems become impossible to ignore, the confused parent attempts to deal with the specific symptom rather than look at the fragmented thinking and child-rearing approaches used. Behavioral modification programs, desensitizing, ignoring, psychotherapy, labeling and finally psychotropic drugs are attempts at changing the symptoms of the problem child instead of directly confronting the problem- poor or little parental training.

The modern-confused parent follows one psychological child-rearing fad after another. These changes in approach appear to the child as if the parent is uncertain, undermining the parental authority and power of the parent. The child assumes the power the parent did not exercise and gradually becomes in charge of raising himself. The permissively raised children remain in this self-centered state and begin to believe that the world really is revolving around them. This egotistical view that "the world owes me a living" cannot take root when the parent is in charge of the family. The parents, by exercising their power, automatically eradicate any self-centered childish notion that anyone owes the child anything.  The child readily learns that the world not only does not revolve around him but also is a complicated and potentially dangerous place.

## VALUE DIFFERENCES

| ESSENTIAL PARENTING | MODERN CONFUSED PARENTING |
|---|---|
| Child will be well behaved, happy helpful, kind, and obedient | Child is not expected to behave: terrible twos, impossible teenagers |
| Child will be observed to fine tune behavior of the child | Child will receive inconsistent messages due to fad experts |
| Child will be trained in specific values, standards | Child receives garbled message due to parental confusion |
| Child will be trained to show concern for the family and community | Child will remain self-centered, "me oriented" |
| Child learns benefits of doing things for others | Child develops the idea that "the world owes me a living" |
| Child is required to use formal interaction with adults | Child is encouraged to use informal interaction with adults,  first name basis |

The rough seas of life can be smoothed through the help and wisdom of a child's parents.  The parent, like the drill sergeant, has a short time to prepare the child or soldier for the battles that lie ahead.  Through knowing the type of thinking and behaviors that the child will need in order to minimize and solve the problems that lie ahead the child can be given the ammunition and armament necessary to be successful in life.  The child who is happy, obedient, helpful, kind and mannerly already has the building blocks necessary for success. The child who has not been trained in these fundamental ways is like a soldier without basic training who is sent to the front to become a casualty.  Self-centered, "me oriented" individuals who think the world owes them a living are destined to alienate others and become frustrated and depressed when they realize the world is not rotating around them.

The untrained, "me oriented" child's rage of not receiving immediate gratification is for the most part directed at his own parents. The confused parents attempt various strategies: appeasing, ignoring, screaming, and surrendering. Providing immediate gratification to the untrained child creates short intervals of peace and increases the illusionary power of the untrained child. The inability of the confused parents, after exhausting all the ideas of the experts to receive an iota of reasonable behavior from their child, eventually reach a point of frustration and anger directed at their child. The parent's sporadic anger is no match for the untrained child, leaving the child by default, the boss of the family.

## POWER DIFFERENCES

| ESSENTIAL PARENTING | MODERN-CONFUSED PARENTING |
|---|---|
| Demonstrates unity and love between parents | Wins favor of child |
| Needs to win all battles with child | Gives in to child |
| Is decisive | Asks child to make decisions |
| Accepts leadership role | Makes the child the boss |
| Is affectionate, loving, smiling playing with child after the child responds to directive | Succumbs to anger and frustration when child does not behave and listen to parents |

Parents must be in charge to allow their child to understand he is not the center of the family or of the universe. By demonstrating their love for each other, the parents nurture the child in the glow of this relationship while also allowing the child to realize he is not always going to be the center of the family unit. The loving, hugging, playing, smiling and sharing with your child are the perks of being a parent and are essential for the happiness of the child. A healthy child needs to know the limits of various stages of life throughout her development so as not to waste her energy and time in determining the limits.

It is the parents who need to define and determine the limits in the family unit. Each parent needs to support the other in upholding these limits to create a clear and precise understanding in the child of what is expected of him. In this way the child is able to focus on the areas of development that are beneficial to him and not waste his time and energy in fighting destructive battles that often are won by neither child nor parent. These useless battles only create angry and frustrated children and parents. The parent, using Purposeful Discipline changes tactics by using a consistent, comprehensive, and relentless war strategy to be undisputedly in charge.

## <u>ESTABLISHING AND MAINTAINING CONTROL</u>

| HOW TO: | HOW NOT TO: |
|---|---|
| Begin with simple command: "no", "stop";"pick up the paper", "come here", "give me your hand" | Negotiate with child, have long verbal discussions of why |
| Discipline consistently | Do not be bothered with discipline |
| Chores are given and increase with age without need for bribes | Parents wait on child, easier to do it myself or bribe with allowances |
| Parents monitor schoolwork | Parents do school work or ignore it |
| Observe the child's behavior to fine tune discipline | Believe experts of the moment in attempting to gain control |

The way to get your "out of control" child back on track is to give direct and simple commands and then be sure they are followed. "Shake my hand", a direct command is insured when you take the child's hand in yours. Each command is expressed in a firm voice and is followed up until it is carried out completely and rapidly without any need for negotiation or discussion. Initially, commands and obedience do require the parent's energy and attention to detail; in the long run this develops habits in the child that make life easier for everyone involved. The commands are extended to more complex daily chores. The chores eventually become internalized and transfer over to the child's other responsibilities such as schoolwork, and ultimately to chosen careers.

Bribing the child through paying him an "allowance" to do family responsibilities gives the child a misleading message. The untrained child is led to believe his parents need him instead of the child needing the family. The untrained child believes schoolwork is done for the benefit of the parent or the teacher instead of for his own benefit. Ultimately the untrained child does not gain the understanding that his eighteen years or so with the family is the golden opportunity to develop the skills, habits and responsibilities the child will need to face the world on his own. This will lead to a turbulent period in young adulthood.

Children use some basic strategies in attempting to control their parents. The following is a list of statements and behaviors used by children to gain control and some <u>Essential Parenting</u>™ counter strategies.

# TYPICAL MANIPULATING RESPONSES AND EP COUNTERS

| STRATEGIES OF CHILDREN ATTEMPTING TO BE IN CONTROL | EP ™ COUNTER STRATEGIES TO MAINTAIN CONTROL |
|---|---|
| 1. " I don't care." "It doesn't bother me." | "Since it doesn't bother you we will increase the time plus take everything away." (Remember to tell the child how much he is missing: "rub salt into the wounds.") |
| 2. Badgering until parents give in | Increase consequences until child realizes you are serious and stops badgering |
| 3. "My friends can do it." | Tell child her friends are not your children. Call friend's parents to find out the truth. |
| 4. "I'll call HRS on you if you spank me." | Call his bluff. Give him the phone. Give consequences for being disrespectful and disloyal. |
| 5. "I hate you!" (Make parent feel guilty) | Tell the child you love her and she will understand when she becomes a parent |
| 6. Tears pouring down | Do not let the tears affect you. When she stops crying discuss the fact the tears are not going to change your decision. |
| 7. Child gives "cold shoulder", does not respond to you. | Time the lack of responding and add it to the time of the consequence. |
| 8. Running away | Refuse to immediately let him back in the house or call police. |
| 9. Stealing from parents | Make pay restitution, verbal or written apology, call police |

## A Measured Level of Fear is Essential in Training

Parents who do not take the time to teach their children how to become independently responsible are robbing the child of the tools necessary for success. Waiting for one's child to develop skills, habits, and responsibilities on her own in the short run may appear to display concern, but in reality it is a shortsighted means of appeasement and pampering. A child needs parents to be in charge to establish the family environment in such a way as to give the child the training needed to face the world head-on without her parents. Imagine a baby bird not prepared by the mother attempting to take off from a perch high up in a tree. This is not a pretty sight, nor is a child without training leaving her family. Either extreme of having too much fear of one's parent or having no fear of the parent leaves the child unprepared for life. A child who has to look over his shoulder in a fearful way means the child has suffered abuse. This child is unable to be sufficiently relaxed to be himself. On the other hand, a child who commits a destructive act and is not fearful of the parent's reactions is either being abusive to the parents or indicating to others the parents did not love him enough to discipline him.

All animals train their offspring to help insure their survival. A mother dog slaps her pups with her paw to redirect the pup's behavior. This is probably due to instinct passed down from antiquity. The pup's fear of the mother's paw sufficiently shapes the pup's behavior while our modern-confused parent thinks that fear is a destructive force to a child's "ego" and must be avoided at all costs. The fear this argument is based on is an exaggerated and abusive use of fear. Extreme fear will be a detriment for training, while a measured use of fear is essential for successful training.

Humans appear to have lost most instinct and rely on a prolonged period of dependency to teach their children cultural knowledge. In many respects our modern society has increased and at the same time decreased this period of dependency. Young and not so young adults live with or return to their parents in their twenties, thirties and beyond prolonging this period. A young child, however, is exposed to aggressiveness, sex, and drugs at an earlier age than ever before through social and media interaction. This exposure comes without a corresponding acceleration in emotional maturity.

Is it necessary for the child to have a healthy respect (fear) of the parent? Fear is the best motivational tool parents have in their arsenal. The tone of voice, the facial expression, the stance of a parent elicits a certain response in a child. A playful voice and smile will encourage the continuation of a particular behavior while a stern voice, piercing eyes and a firm stance will intimidate a child into changing the offensive behavior. Approximately eighty five to ninety percent of all adult communication is non-verbal and the younger the child the greater the impact of the non-verbal segment of communication and the less the impact of the verbal part of communication.

The younger the child, the easier it is to intimidate her. Obviously it is easier to sculpture and establish control of a child's behavior and thought processes at this early and sensitive stage of development. If parents ignore this sensitive period when the child can learn readily how to behave in a reasonable manner it often leads to the option of using drugs- Ritalin, Prozac, etc., to control the child's behavior later on. There are only two ways of controlling an individual **against** their will: intimidation and drugs.

Our society has moved away from the physical intimidation of spanking or slapping the hand of a young child and has replaced with a vengeance, controlling by drugs. The United States uses 90% or five times more Ritalin than the entire rest of the world combined. In addition, the pharmaceutical companies are currently promoting new generations of Prozac and Paxil for children. Controlling a child through drugs freezes the child's emotional development. There is no need for emotional coping skills, the drug manages the emotions and, at times, even the thoughts.

When a parent uses a subtle form of intimidation when the child is young such as a deep voice, "evil eye", picking up a wooden spoon, to get a young child to change his behavior, it can be done without straight jacketing the child's emotions. If the parents do a poor job of explaining the rationale behind their being upset, resentment can fester. However, the child's interaction with the parents who poorly implement this disciplining responsibility is not as devastating to his emotional development as are drugs. Drugs are adjusted or altered to resolve any emotional problems while the child is a passive bystander. There is no opportunity to learn to alter one's emotions by changing ones thinking and behavior.

It is widely accepted in mental health circles that an individual's emotional development remains at the age when the person started on drugs- street or prescribed- unless they were given the added dimension of psychotherapeutic counseling. A man of the chronological age of 45 who started drugs at ten-years-old remains at that emotional age. The emotional arresting of the child is a heavy price to pay by the child so the parent does not have to get off the couch to discipline. When parents take their time and energy to discipline their child it is an act of concern and love. Choosing an appropriate level of fear in order to motivate the child to do the reasonable thing is neither traumatic nor abusive. The child realizes the parents are serious about eliminating a particular behavior or situation. The child complies with the forceful stance the parents have taken. Thus, there is no need for further use of escalated force that could cross the line into abuse.

It is precisely because of the introduction of an appropriate level of intimidation at the right moment that the situation does not become a prolonged battle increasing the potential for abuse. Fear is a powerful, if not the most powerful, motivator for change that parents have in their arsenal, but has to be coupled with a parent-child discussion to insure a positive outcome. The discussion should be about the reasons why the initial behavior was inappropriate and the appropriate behaviors the parent expects in similar situations in the future. As the child complies with the parents' expected behavior the parents will have greater opportunity to display the playful response to the child's parentally sanctioned behavior. The child will focus more on behaviors that will be approved by parents and less on searching for the extreme limits of unacceptable behavior to test their parent's resolve and love.

## Discipline, Not Permissiveness, Is True Unconditional Love

Parents are being brainwashed by psychobabble to eliminate all forms of creating fear from their discipline bag: the fear of a spanking, the use of the stern non-verbal communication (evil eye), the withholding of affection (cold shoulder), and even "time out." They have been instructed to replace fear with bribery, material rewards, and the ultimate anti-training slogan of cultural relativism- "unconditional love".

Parental love should not be conditional depending on attributes such as appearance, intelligence or physical abilities of one child compared to another. All children regardless of their attributes or their defects should be loved without arbitrary conditions. It is true parents ought to love without reservation the gift God gave them, their children. Unconditional love has come to mean unconditional acceptance of all behaviors of the child regardless of the social appropriateness and moral implications of the behavior. This distortion of the concept of unconditional love by the cultural relativists has become the rationale for the permissive child rearing approach in the United States. If you truly love your child, the rationale implies, you need to stop imposing your values on your child and accept the child's untrained, uncensored, and self-centered expressions of behavior as a confirmation of parental love for the child.

The unconditional love/permissiveness concept attempts to justify the avoiding of the difficult responsibilities and choices of a truly loving parent. In essence the unconditional love/ permissiveness concept robs our children of parental guidance in an age of numerous difficult choices. Allowing children to make their own choices without guidance is not a sign of love but, a confirmation of a parent's relinquishing a major component of the expression of love: discipline. In fact, the parents are entrusted to teach their children good from bad behavior. The teaching or training of a child is a primary sign of love. Allowing a child to continue on a destructive path is not a sign of unconditional love. It is at least a sign of laziness and at worst a sign of not caring. All mammals train their offspring. For human parents to abandon this function is to significantly increase the probability of the child's failure as an adult, which tends to increase the probability of future chaos reigning in society.

## PROS AND CONS OF BEING IN CHARGE

| WHY TO BE IN CHARGE | WHY NOT TO: |
|---|---|
| For protection | Make the child like you better |
| Make life manageable | In order not to be bothered with incident |
| Have emotionally healthy child | Pacify child |

When you pacify a child you temporarily eliminate the problem. The parent loses an opportunity to train the child and the child loses the moral lesson. The undisciplined child has less of a reservoir of knowledge to deal with the next problem that arises. The disciplined child, on the other hand, knows his parents will be there to teach and discipline him in the many incidents that will unfold in life. The lessons and skills taught by parents help to shield children from the chaos and arbitrariness of normal life.

## Start Training: As Soon As Necessary (ASAN)

The process of Purposeful Discipline should begin as soon as necessary, which is when the child exhibits behavior the parent does not feel is appropriate. This may occur as young as two or three months of age when the nursing baby bites the mother's nipple, or screams for no reason. For the children's safety, the word "No!" must be taught as soon as they begin to explore the world around them. The earlier the intervention, the easier it is to obtain results with the minimum of effort. "Nipping it in the bud" pays large dividends in child rearing.

The observation of the child's behavior and thinking will determine the speed and complexity of the Purposeful Discipline process. When children display immature thinking PD immediately attempts to enhance their thinking. The following lists gives the child's immature thinking and the PD instructions that will create a more responsible thinking pattern.

### INCREASE MATURE THINKING

| "CHILD'S IMMATURE THINKING | PD TECHNIQUES TO ENHANCE THINKING |
|---|---|
| I can't attitude: "I can't do it." "I can't help it." | Encourage child to do. "You can do it if you think you can." Begin as early as possible. "I can do anything if I try." Break down tasks to basic parts. Independence. |
| Victimization: "He did it." "I couldn't help it." | Investigate incidents. Get him to admit his responsibility in the action. See Chapter 4 |
| Lack of empathy. Insensitive to the impact of his behavior of others. | Connect child's pain with the pain of others. See Empathy Training. |
| Irresponsible thinking. "I forgot to do my chores, schoolwork." | "Forget" to do something for the child and then explain the importance of being dependable. |
| Lying. Insists she is telling the truth when you caught her "red-handed." | Give her forced choice of a positive consequence for telling the truth and a negative consequence for continuing to insist she is right. |

| | |
|---|---|
| Stealing: takes something and insists it is hers. | Take something of hers and say it is yours and discuss her feelings at this turn of events. |
| Unrealistic expectations. "I am going to be an astrophysicist or pass a test without studying." | Spell out how to become a physicist and note behavior that is needed to be changed- studying very hard. |
| Irresponsible: Blames others when things go wrong. | Show him how to define the problem and how to solve it realistically. |
| Prideful: Refuses to admit when wrong. | Teach him mistakes are fundamental to learning reality. |
| Short range thinking. "I didn't realize what would happen." | Encourage child to set goals and work towards them, Give appropriate consequence. |
| Supersensitive: " The world is against me. It is unfair." | Teach to realize the world is unfair and only through hard work can you attain your goals. |

## Never Miss An Opportunity to Discipline

Discipline can take place anywhere it is safe and convenient for the parent and child. When a discipline situation is begun, enough time should be anticipated and allowed for successful completion of the lesson. Parents should attempt to anticipate the child's acting out behavior and descriptively allow the child to know the specific consequences the child will face for inappropriate behavior. The parents need to follow through on their work.

A child often appears to sense when the parent is at a disadvantage such as being on the phone, in a friend or relative's home or in a public area. In this type of situation the child frequently tests the parental limits. When disciplining is necessary in a public arena, the discipline should be quiet and unobtrusive relating the consequence for the inappropriate behavior. If the issue is not sufficiently resolved then, the child can be informed that "we will deal with this when we get home." This allows the child to reflect on and worry about his inappropriate behavior and the pending consequences.

63

When a child is young, structure, rituals and routines insure an external organization when imposed on the child that leads to mental health: a time to rise, a time to eat, play, work and sleep. This structure enables us to regulate ourselves physically, emotionally and mentally. During each day there should be specific times for brushing teeth, taking a bath, getting ready for bed to increase efficiency and decrease unnecessary discussion. Routines make life's daily activities automatic, eliminating many potential conflicts.

To be disciplined one has to have a purpose. The purpose can be as mundane as getting to school on time or as elaborate as being a good family member or citizen of the United States. The purpose will dictate the standards and rules (setting limits). These rules and standards need to be consistently upheld for the individual to be reminded of the behaviors that will help obtain their goal or purpose. If the standards are not adhered to, there must be consequences that follow. The child realizes that conforming to the standards and rules and working for the goal has short-term acceptance by the members of the family and long term benefits of approaching or reaching the objective. As individuals complete more and more objectives, they develop the habits necessary to internalize a disciplined approach to life.

A child has to reach many milestones such as expressing and feeding oneself, toilet training, giving up pacifiers and bottles, learning to walk, beginning reading and listening. Each milestone reached places the child closer to becoming a functioning adult, while each one delayed jeopardizes the smooth transition into adulthood. The undisciplined child has a rocky road ahead with many detours that could end in an unfulfilled and difficult life. The Purposeful Discipline trained parent shows the truest expression of love by acting to give their children the best possible future.

We hear many incredible and numerous excuses by parents concerning their child's inappropriate behavior. "My child didn't have a nap", "is ill", "is nervous", "we moved about a month ago, and he is unsettled", " her grandfather died", " he is affected by the divorce". As the parent makes these pronouncements they almost never take the opportunity to discipline the child. You almost never hear direct commands like "Sit back in the chair", "shake hands", and "don't slap me". Instead the excuses come and the inappropriate behavior is ignored. Direct commands by the parent to the child that are correctly followed are clear signs that the parents have behavioral expectations and have begun the process of training their child. Making excuses and ignoring inappropriate behavior is a clear sign that parents have no clue that discipline is a sequential process that needs to be consistently and constantly enforced to gain best and most rapid results.

The results of training a child to listen and follow parental authority are positively wonderful. A toddler who listens to a parent's commands (clear and precise limits) -"stop", "don't touch the stove", "stay here" is much safer than a child who does what he wants in today's fast paced world. The child in a family that has completed <u>Essential Parenting</u>™ training understands where his or her place is in the family. <u>EP</u> families know that bed time and eating times, destruction of property, hurting oneself or others, respecting others and following commands for safety are non negotiable issues, but are decisions made solely by the adults not influenced nor manipulated by the child. In essence the child receives the parent's commitment to love and discipline fostering the child's blossoming into a healthy adult.

**Missed Opportunities to Discipline- Fertile Ground for ADD/ADHD Being Consistently in Charge  the Antidote**

The modern-confused parents do not want to traumatize their child by being decisive and dogmatic in their decision making.  These misguided parents set no limits and have no definite parameters for anything: bedtime, eating, and potty training schedules are negotiated daily with their child.  There are no definitive behavioral expectations for the child since the child may be tired, sick, or unsettled.  A predetermined consequence such as losing a privilege, time out, or being slapped on the behind is too potentially harmful to their child.  Therefore the child is never certain of the consequences or the clear and precise rules of his environment.

Not creating a consistent environment for one's child leaves a vacuum where the child gains control establishing a world that better meets his needs.  When a child is not taught the precise and clear limits he pushes and pulls to determine the limits.  As the pushing increases without any counter force from the parents, the child gains greater and greater control.  The child begins to believe and feel that he has more power than he really does and acts as if he is in charge or, at the very least, no adult can tell him what to do or how to do it.

The abdication of the traditional parental role by the modern-confused parent has led to children who think and feel they are and really appear to be in control of their families.  A child who believes he is in control has a burden placed on his shoulders before he has the maturity and strength to successfully handle it.  It is not fair for the parent to accept the child's futile attempt of carrying the family's weight, knowing it will hurt or even crush the child.  The child in control faces problems of control outside of the family with peers, family, friends and school authorities. The modern-confused child-rearing approach creates a child who is constantly pushing his outer world of self-centeredness without getting a clear answer from his parents as to where his personal world ends and the family and society begins.

Parents who have abdicated their traditional role by pampering the child are doing their child a disservice of not developing frustration tolerance. It appears many modern-confused parents are able to create a fantasy in their child's mind that she can do anything she wants to do anytime she wants to do it. Going outside of the family eventually puts an end to this nonsensical fantasy. Daycare or school may be the first time a child steps out from under the protective umbrella of the parent. Childcare workers, preschool and elementary teachers and coaches cannot continue the hoax that a particular child is the center of the universe. Teachers need students to follow directions in order for the group to function in a purposeful way. When a child does "his own thing" producing some form of chaos in a group, the authorities step in. "Your child must leave the program", "your child must be screened developmentally", "your child is failing this grade", "your child needs to be on Ritalin" are heard loud and clear by the modern-confused parent.

The epidemic of ADD/ADHD (Attention Deficit Disorder/Attention Deficit Hyperactive Disorder) children is the result of confused parents not training their children to listen. Instead confused parents are doing one or more of the following:

- Being inconsistent in following up the behavioral demands made on child.
- Pampering the child or doing the child's work instead of teaching the child and insisting the child do for himself.

- Accepting the child's outrageous behavioral demands without any real resistance.

In each case the child does not have to worry about the parental reaction to his behavior. In the first case, the child realizes that his parent "barks without a bite" and soon learns to ignore the parental outbursts. The screamer-barker appears tough to the outsider but the child plays with this "paper tiger." In the second case, the pampering parent makes the child expect the world to service him. When other adults such as teachers in school require the child to do something, the child waits for someone to do it for him. In the third case, the obnoxious outbursts are not tolerated outside of the parent's influence and are the cause of many confrontations with authorities. In each case the child is not taught the skills necessary to listen and comply with the reasonable requests of other adults. What are readily acceptable limits to a traditionally raised child become a potential conflict with a child not trained in obedience.

A child following parental directions is learning to listen. Listening is a skill that is necessary in school, in one's profession, and all throughout life. A parent being consistently in charge teaching the child to pay attention is the antidote to developing an ADD/ADHD child. Through listening and following directions of parental figures a child learns the social norms of his culture. Asking permission before leaving the house or before taking someone else's possessions are expected behaviors of society. Manners and social graces fall into this category of social norms. As a child learns social expectations, she loses a portion of her infantile self-centeredness and gains the perspective of a functioning member of her family and society in general. The child's acceptance of her evolving status to eventual adulthood along with the required incremental increases in expected responsible behavior is a sign of a healthy developing individual which prevents schools, mental health professionals and medical "experts" from using their credentials to label your child ADD/ADHD.

## The Reality of the Compliant and Noncompliant Child

The "permissive experts" would like us to believe that the obedient child will be a non-thinking, conformist robot, while the untrained, non-compliant child will be a critical thinking person with creativity. The reality of the last forty years has demonstrated that the non-compliant child has a greater need to conform than the compliant child does with members outside the family. The need to belong is basic to humans. When the child does not have the security of belonging to a stable family, he will reach out for some other group to belong. In the past forty years some of the groups that have preyed upon untrained children have included hippies, druggies, religious cults, gangs, and communes.

When these children untrained in reality choose to act inappropriately, other authorities from outside the family step in and place them in groups. The United States medical establishment has created and sanctioned ADD/ADHD, Defiant Oppositional Disorder, Conduct Disorder, and Major Depression Disorder which categorizes a child and develops an artificial identity that forces the child into an involuntary group. Children diagnosed with these psychiatric disorders may receive a false sense of belonging when interacting with others who have been given the same diagnosis but at the cost of being segregated from normal children. Thus, they do not observe socially approved behavior which ends up accentuating their problem rather than addressing their deficiencies through the process of compensation.

Only the parents of children with mental disorders profit from this psychiatric process of labeling. The child receives the total stigma while the child-rearing of the parents is removed from the equation. The label instantly makes the child responsible for his untrained, inappropriate behavior rather than examining the entire family interaction, especially the parents in this child-rearing process. It is as if the psychiatric establishment wants to believe that a child has the wherewithal to raise himself and parents have no impact on the shaping of the child's behavior.

On the other hand, the compliant child who has profited from a close bond with her parents in the socialization process naturally reaches the stage where the individual leaves the nest to strike out on her own to start her own family. The skills and knowledge learned from parents as well as internalization of rules and expectations put in place the necessary building blocks for independent, responsible and critical thought. These better-trained individuals are less vulnerable to the pressures of joining a dangerous peer group since the individual belongs to the most intimate group, a family. Upon leaving the childhood family, the maturing individual proceeds to use her past experiences to build a new and better version of her ideal family.

## The Importance of Parents Regaining Control

Even with a non-judgmental culture and "dumbing down" of standards, authorities are making important decisions concerning our children. Despite lowered standards of acceptable behavior and some of our public schools placing as many as 70% of students on the honor role to appease parents, eventually some form of exclusion becomes a reality. These exclusions include: suspension from school, removal from the team, a low SAT score, not getting accepted to the college of their choice, expulsion from college for not maintaining good enough grades.

A child should not be handed everything she wants. She needs to work for what she gets and at times fail to get what she wants because this is reality. Developing the ability to handle frustration (not getting what you want when you want it) is to be given the tools necessary for success in the real world. We ought to protect our children from evil when they are too young to fight their own battles. At the same time it is the responsibility of the parent to train the child in coping skills: critical thinking, appropriate decision making, physical toughness, turning a negative into a positive, functioning in an unfair and an often brutal world. Thus, parents must have the authority and courage to be able to deny the desires of their child.

When the parents take charge and place themselves back on the top of the organizational chart, the entire family benefits. The child no longer wastes his energy and the parent's time attempting to control his parents and is able to put his focus into developing necessary skills which will allow him to be successful now and in his future life. The parents are able to use their energies to train and enjoy their children instead of putting out behavioral "fires" created by their undisciplined children.

When the modern-confused parents attempt to regain control by pointing out the child's inappropriate behavior the child changes the subject, poses as a victim, or attacks the integrity of the parent. The child's accusation throws the parents into a defensive mode thereby allowing the child to escape any consequence for his misdeed. The parents become exhausted, forgetting the reason for the confrontation or throwing up their hands in frustration. This allows the child by default to be the victor. The child is emboldened by this aggressive manipulative attack strategy's success becoming a tenacious warrior who will control the family agenda instead of the parent being in control.

The parents must realize that they need to regain control or their child will be victorious in parental confrontation while being social misfits in society. Once the parents realize that their abdication of power has created this self-destructive, out-of-control child, the parents will be ready for changing this pattern. Through <u>Essential Parenting</u>™, the parents will take responsibility for raising their child instead of pretending that the child can accomplish successful adulthood miraculously on his own. There are techniques and strategies passed down from generation to generation that are applicable to our present time. The knowledge of child-rearing is essential for parents to be responsible, in charge, and in command of their family.

# Chapter 4

## Loving Through Purposeful Discipline

*"Spare the rod and spoil the child" is a corruption of the proverb. "He that spareth his rod hateth his son." Proverbs 13:24.*

The message is powerful, parents who do not put effort into disciplining their children hate their children, not merely spoil them. The undisciplined child will develop destructive behavioral patterns that will hurt himself as well as others. On the other hand the disciplined child will learn constructive methods that will assist him in his interacting with the world.

Purposeful Discipline is a demonstration of one person's love for another. When parents intentionally discipline their child to alter a destructive behavior, the parents are expressing love towards their child. When parents ignore or appease their child's negative behavior, the parents are under the false assumption that these are positive strategies. It is true that if a parent conscientiously ignores a specific negative behavior for an excessive number of times, the behavior will become extinguished. The problem is the parent's frustration may appear in their body language, facial expressions, or voice, which prolongs the extinguishing process, making it unworkable. Appeasing the child with material goods only escalates the negative behavior making it counter productive to the development of a healthy, unspoiled child. The figure below shows the foundation of purposeful discipline:

## PURPOSEFUL DISCIPLINE TEACHES TRADITIONAL VALUE

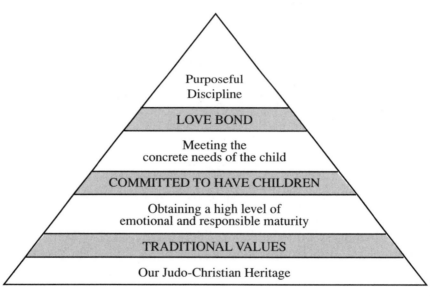

The reason for Purposeful Discipline is for the parent to intentionally provide the child with teaching or training that will assist her in developing traditional values and behaviors. These traditional values and behaviors have passed the test of time and have been proven to be effective in developing a healthy individual. Providing the child with values such as love, obedience, respectfulness, empathy, honesty, independence, will power, conscience, critical thinking, pain control, social skills, and safety awareness is an expression of love. Parents who consciously pass on their wisdom through Purposeful Discipline will eventually create a child who is internalizing the process of becoming self-disciplined. The emergence of a young individual's self-discipline is a sure sign of parental love for the child.

## Parents Need to be Responsible and Emotionally Mature

In order to start the process of Purposeful Discipline; parents need to have arrived at a point in life where they are ready to relinquish their self-centeredness, and become concerned for others. This attainment of responsible emotional maturity is a prerequisite for healthy human interaction especially with children. Adults, in the role of parents, have the power to create or ignore the child's emotional, social, and moral development. This crucial role of parenting should only begin when adults have responsible emotional maturity in order to assist the child's development rather than exploit the child for their own selfish needs. The accomplished person using PD needs to possess the awareness and emotional maturity to appreciate the wonderful opportunity they have to pass on true, positive values that will be a guiding force for those they touch.

## Parents Bond with their Children by Meeting their Concrete Physical Needs

The parent reaching out to the child assisting him to meet his needs is the fundamental basis of a parent's love for a child. Holding, touching, feeding, sheltering, and clothing the child are necessary for the child to physically survive. As the parents meet more and more needs, the parents and children develop an emotional bond which is commonly called "love." This is like putting money in the bank that you can withdraw when necessary in order to place the child back on the right track without worrying about traumatizing the child.

## Essential Parenting™ Actively Teaches Through Purposeful Discipline

Human infants need to learn the correct thinking and behavior patterns in order to be accepted and to flourish in a complex cultural world that is distinctly human. The ultimate reason for Purposeful Discipline is to assist a child on his journey through the cultural world by intentionally teaching or training him. In other words, the basic needs stage of love is elevated to the more abstract stage of love by the parents imparting the wisdom gained during their lifetime to the life of the young child for better functioning in an intricate culture.

In the same manner we meet the basic physical needs of an infant such as touching, giving food, water, and warmth, parents should, As Soon As Needed (ASAN) begin the teaching and training of the child. Purposeful Discipline starts when parents, through the observation of their infant's behavior, realize parental influence is needed to help the development of the child. By beginning ASAN the child is establishing healthy behavioral patterns which create the foundation for opening up opportunities for more elaborate patterns of healthy behavior. By establishing these patterns when a child is young and malleable the parental sculpturing process is more effortless. This results in more significant progress than waiting for the individual to age into adolescence and harden. At this late stage the sculpturing process becomes a "tough love" that is slower and much more difficult.

### Purposeful Discipline Requires Firmness

This Purposeful Discipline (PD) process is not for the faint hearted or lazy soul. Initially the responsible individual using PD has to provide the energy to begin the process and the resolve to stay with it. As the positive results shown by the child become evident, the process itself energizes the responsible adult and removes any doubt the child may have created in the mind of the parent about

76

the effectiveness of Purposeful Discipline. If the disciplining starts at the infant or toddler stage and is sufficiently forceful, the child will be convinced joining the parent is the best strategy. In a similar fashion a hostage often blindly follows or even falls in love with the hostage taker, the child following a firm encounter with justified discipline will want to sit in the lap of the disciplining parent affectionately telling how much he loves them.

If the discipline starts later in the preschool stage or the discipline effort is either inconsistent or irresolute, then the child may verbally or non verbally act as if the Purposeful Discipline is abusive rather than an act of love. "You are doing this for yourself," "You don't love me," "I hate you!" are frequent responses of a child in the beginning stages of PD. The adult should tell the child "I am doing this because I do love you." The adult following PD informs the child the immediate and long-term purpose of his actions. "I am teaching you in this area to eventually make life easier for you." As long as the child realizes the adult is doing the PD to aid the child they will not become resentful. When the discipline's purpose is to improve the life of the child then it is an act of love. It is for this reason that the adult has to reach an emotional mental and spiritual maturity to practice Purposeful Discipline.

## Essential Parenting Utilizes the Purposeful Discipline Process to Effectively and Efficiently Inculcate Traditional Values in the Child

## The Purposeful Discipline Process Has Eight Steps

    A    Role model traditional values.
    B    Be in charge
    C    Communicate parameters
    D    Set limits and expectations
    E    Prepare child with anticipated consequences
    F    De-brief after the event
    G    Administer consequences
    H    Discuss purpose of the discipline.

## A.  Role Model Traditional Values

Adults who are ready to be parents possess awareness and
emotional maturity as well as know the behavior and thought
patterns their children need to have to be morally productive
people in their future.  These ideal behaviors and thought patterns
serve to motivate the parents by giving them a specific objective to
get the child's initially inappropriate behavior or thoughts to
resemble the parent's ideal.  Through role modeling traditional
behavior and successive attempts at teaching and or training, the
parents decrease the discrepancy through the sculpturing process
between the initially inappropriate behavior or thought and the
ideal behavior.

These ideal patterns in <u>Essential Parenting</u>™ are the traditional
values that are the bedrock of our culture.  For parents to begin the
process of instilling traditional values in the mind of the child, the
parents need to believe in these values, to agree with each other
these values are positive for the development of the child, and
most importantly role model these values and behaviors.  The
parents differing on a set of values will invariably cause some
level of confusion for the child, while two parents agreeing on the
values will increase the probability that the values will be
internalized.

| TRADITIONAL VALUES IDEAL VALUES THOUGHTS AND BELIEFS | = | PARAMETERS "ROLE MODELED" AND TAUGHT TO CHILD |
|---|---|---|

## B.  Be In Charge: Allow Natural Fear to Foster Respect

Parents who are "in charge" allow natural fear to foster respect.
Your child is your solemn responsibility to raise.  The child is not
your friend or your equal.  To become a friend or equal to the child
the parent has to consciously distort reality.  The much larger

parent with a deeper voice, stronger body, control of the financial resources, is a giant to a small child. Parents, who play the phony game of "I'm your equal," lose their authority as parents. The child trained by permissive/materialistic parents usually responds in a more socially appropriate manner when confronted by a traditional adult than she does with her own parents.

The child instinctively fears a much larger, older and more powerful adult. The child's natural fear of the adult motivates the child to be on her best behavior. It is for this reason many children who are unruly in the presence of their parents behave much better when they are with someone else. All respect is based on a certain level of fear. The cold shoulder/fear of losing the affection of the parent, grandparent, teacher, friend, motivates most individuals to remain on or get back on track. The fear of getting a speeding ticket keeps most of us respectful of the posted speed limits. The fear of low grades, dismissal, or loss of privileges serves as motivation for most of us in educational and employment settings.

Removing the rational fear of a child for a parent/authority figure is the surest way to develop a vulnerable, mentally weak, socially maladaptive child. Fear is a powerful if not the most powerful motivator in socializing people. For the parent to throw away natural fear is the best method a parent has to insure future problems for the child. Natural fear is the foundation of a child listening to a parent. Remove the natural fear of the child for his parent or other authority figure and witness the erosion of the power of the adult.

C. Communicate Parameters

After parents reach agreement with each other on the values and expectations they desire in their child, the parents create parameters. A parameter is the defining of the expected general value to be internalized by the child. "Good people are kind." "You will be a kind person." "Cleanliness is next to Godliness." "Personal hygiene is important in our family." You only make one first impression. "Look at Jimmy, how distinguished he looks all dressed up in a suit." Parents through their communication with their children establish the parameters of a value, that is, laden pictures they want their children to internalize. The more creative energy the parents use in various situations to communicate these parameters, the clearer and more focused the child's picture is in his head of what the parents expect from the child. Both parents working together develop focused values and expectations for the child to internalize.

D. Set Limits and Expectations

Parents set limits and expectations when they state the rules of what the child can and cannot do. As the parents observe the child's behavior, the parent realizes that the child often wanders outside of the established parameters. The child might bite a sibling, not share toys, or hit the dog with a stick. The parent sees the discrepancy between the parameter (desired value) and the child's inappropriate behavior. To move the child back inside the lines of the parameter, the parents announce to the child the rules of what the child can and cannot do. In other words, set limits and expectations. "You will not bite your sister," "you will share toys," "you will pet the dog, not hit him." These limits and expectations will bring the child back into the boundaries of being a kind person. In the same manner, the expectation of brushing teeth daily at 7:30pm before taking a bath, and combing hair before school helps keep the child inside the parameters of good personal hygiene. The limits and expectations work to anchor the child into a particular parameter that assists the child in living the value the parents know is best for the child. The figure below demonstrates how parameters are comprised of limits and expectations:

| PARAMETERS ARE COMPRISED OF: LIMITS AND EXPECTATIONS | | | |
|---|---|---|---|
| Does not take from others | Redo it until it is right | | |
| | Take initiative | Set Goals | |
| The greater the effort The greater the reward | | Concentrate | |
| | Follow through | | |
| **WORK ETHIC** | | | |

Once the limits and expectations are announced there is absolutely no negotiation that should take place with the child. Parents have the experience and knowledge necessary to develop the specific rules and regulations to direct the child on the right path to socially approved values and actions. Children lack the experiential prerequisites to set their own limits and to pretend differently is not only a waste of time, but will lead to continual power struggles. The child allowed to negotiate one limit will tend to try to negotiate <u>all</u> limits until the parent stops this pointless negotiating charade by putting her foot down.

Parents consistently enforcing the set limits decrease the child testing the limits. Inconsistent enforcement of the limits increases the tendency of a child to test the limits. A child will stop testing limits by negotiating as soon as the child learns the parents will not tolerate this nonsense. Parents reach this point by using adequate follow-through with adequate consequences. Upon realizing that opening up her mouth to attempt to re-negotiate the limits only results in increasingly stiffer consequences, the child will rapidly put an end to her shenanigans. When a child realizes "you mean what you say" your respect and credibility increase in her eyes and the tendency to test the limits decreases to a screeching halt.

As the parents follow up by enforcing the limits and expectations, the child will begin to internalize the stated limits and expectations. The internalizing of limits and expectations allows everyone to prosper. The parent is able to have the security the child will exhibit socially appropriate behavior patterns. The child knows the parents will remain pleased as long as the child abides by the rules. The compliant child, most importantly, is open to learn from his parent and is free to creatively experiment with new behaviors without the anxiety of angering his parents. He also does not waste his precious time and energy doing random behaviors for the sole purpose of eliciting a reaction from his parents. The compliant child knows to ask the parent for clarification when he is uncertain, rather than recklessly acting before thinking of the reality consequences of his impulsive behavior.

How to Set Limits and Expectations

• *Role model appropriate traditional behavior.*

Parents role modeling appropriate behavior allow the child to imitate the behavior the parent desires. The role modeling unconsciously creates the picture of the desired values (parameters) and do's and don'ts (limits and expectations) in the child's head.
• *Be in charge and teach the child the word "NO".*

Setting limits starts with teaching the child to stop when you say the word "NO". If a child does not automatically respond to the command "No", the child will have a mind set to push the limits for no other reason than to test the resolve of the authority figure. The game becomes "I will attempt behaviors to see the reaction of the adult." The focus is on the adult's reaction rather than on learning about other important aspects of reality. A child who has internalized the concept of "NO" is free to explore her environment within the established limits without the burden of having to continually test the limits.

The obedient child can interact with the adult in a cooperative manner optimizing the instruction and assistance in learning lessons from the surrounding environment. Spending time with the compliant child is a pleasure for the parent while the child enjoys the benefits of receiving encouragement and love necessary for healthy development. On the other hand, the untrained "brat" is a high maintenance individual, needing constant supervision to protect property, himself, and others. The constant behavioral battles deprive the child of encouragement from the parent.

- *Set limits that will be enforced and have expectations that are reasonable.*

Limits that are not consistently monitored and enforced are worse than not setting them in the first place. Any transgression not enforced leads to a further discrepancy of the adult setting the limits and places into question all limits. Expectations need to be realistic to motivate the child without unnecessary frustration.

- *Parents unite in stating agreed upon limits and expectations.*

Only after parents reach a consensus on the limits they want to set for their child should they announce the limits. These limits are stated clearly and precisely to the child. The child then repeats the limits stated to them.

- *Parents follow-up and follow-through using consequences.*

Parents need to follow their child with their eyes to know if the child is obeying the limits. This visual follow-up is required to evaluate the adherence to the set limits. (See POISE process) The follow-through with rewards or punishing consequences internalizes the limits for the child.

E. Prepare Child with Anticipated Consequences and Forced Choices

Once the parameters and corresponding limits are set, situational preparation logically follows. The particular situation that is going to occur such as visiting relatives, going to church, taking a day trip, requires that the parents prepare the children as to their specific expectations. Parents need to give the child the anticipation of a reward or punishing consequence for appropriate or inappropriate behavior. By spelling out the parent's expectations to the child, the parents are setting up a forced choice that increases the probability of the child displaying the socially approved behavior. Consider the following example of outlining expectations.

"We are going to Aunt Minnie's house in the morning and if you sit correctly and speak respectfully when someone asks you a question, we will go to the beach in the afternoon. However, if you misbehave, we will go straight home and you will sit on a chair in the kitchen for the afternoon."
When the parents prepare the children of the family as to the plan for the day, the expectations and anticipation of positive or punishing consequences for appropriate and inappropriate behavior, the children receive a clear and precise picture of what the parents want. This forced choice is a powerful means of shaping a child's behavior. After all, an individual will usually choose a rewarding consequence over a punishing consequence.

F. Debrief After the Event

After the specific event the parents de-brief the children on how things went according to their perception. The children were forewarned by the prepping, and should be evaluated immediately following the situational event.

The children know that if they sat and behaved correctly they would go to the beach, but if they misbehaved they would go straight home and sit on the chair. The parents inform the child that the behavior the child chose was his responsibility to reap the reward or punishment. This procedure, if done correctly, will place responsibility with the child and eliminate the child from blaming the parent.

## G.  Administer Consequences

Parents need to observe the child and give rewarding or punishing consequences depending on the behavior exhibited. Consequences are responses to behavior that increase or decrease the probability of a person continuing a particular behavior. Rewards, or positive consequences, increase the probability while punishments, or negative consequences, decrease the probability of a person adhering to a specific behavior. Using consequences shows the determination of an adult to enforce their limits and maintain the integrity as parental authority figures.

This process eliminates the child having a legitimate argument to blame the parents. The parents through prepping their children with the anticipatory consequences have only to administer the consequence already mapped out for the appropriate or inappropriate behavior. Administering pre-selected consequences solidifies the credibility of the parents by keeping their word. This allows the children to realize they made a choice that involved positive or negative repercussions with which they will have to live. (See following section on consequences)

## H.  Discuss the Purpose of the Discipline

Finally, the parents will ask the children or tell them the reason for the discipline in order to increase the understanding and decrease resentment. "We are at the beach because you did a great job being respectful at Aunt Minnie's house" or "you are sitting in the chair because you chose disrespectful behavior." Depending upon the age of the child, the parent explains how his choices affect the family, friends and his own development as a person. The younger the child, the more simple the explanation. The older the child the more complex the explanation of the reason for the specific consequence.

A young child up to two years old may receive a slap on the behind or hand for biting another child. The parent needs to say as they administer the slap "Don't bite, it hurts Johnny," in a very firm tone. The child should be asked to tell you why he received the slap. He needs to repeat that biting Johnny is bad because it hurts him. The child needs to state "I will not bite again."

The four year old child involved in a biting incident needs to receive an immediate punishing consequence sufficiently severe enough to give genuine pain, not a love tap that encourages rather than discourages the inappropriate behavior. After the punishing consequence is administered, the older the child the more elaborate and graphic the discussion of the misbehavior. You can talk about the bacteria in the mouth infecting the other child, making him bleed and causing him great pain. The more graphically detailed the greater the impact on the child.

## There are Two Types of Consequences

**Natural Consequences** which directly result from reality

**Human Imposed Consequences**, which are composed of:
Reward- positive consequence that increase the probability of behavior occurring again
Punishment –adverse consequences that decrease the probability of the behavior occurring again

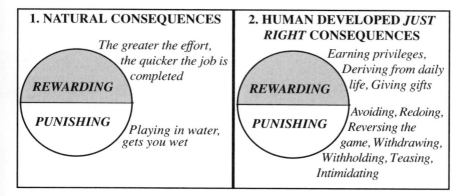

| 1. NATURAL CONSEQUENCES | 2. HUMAN DEVELOPED *JUST RIGHT* CONSEQUENCES |
|---|---|
| REWARDING — *The greater the effort, the quicker the job is completed* | REWARDING — *Earning privileges, Deriving from daily life, Giving gifts* |
| PUNISHING — *Playing in water, gets you wet* | PUNISHING — *Avoiding, Redoing, Reversing the game, Withdrawing, Withholding, Teasing, Intimidating* |

## Natural Consequences

There are natural consequences that teach us about reality. If we do not eat we get hungry. Hunger naturally follows not eating. If we run into a boulder we get hurt. If we do not drink liquids, we get thirsty. Thirst is the natural consequence of not drinking liquids. As many college students learn drinking alcohol and not sleeping for long periods of time makes one tired and vulnerable to illness. Parents should allow their child to experience natural consequences as long as they do not pose an imminent danger to the child. It teaches the child directly about life. Essential Parenting™ encourages parents to make use of natural consequences because of their power to directly teach reality. However, our function as parents to protect our offspring rightly prevents us from allowing our child to suffer many natural consequences.

## Human Imposed Consequences

Humans have the power to think. They reward or punish a behavior they like or dislike according to their value system. Through this process of rewards and punishments humans create their culture.

## Rewarding Consequences

A rewarding consequence administered by the parent increases the likelihood that the child will repeat the behavior. In most cases a reward of a pat on the back, verbal praise, a gift or prize, special food, or increased autonomy will increase the probability of a person doing the behavior again.

There are three categories of Rewarding Consequences.
Earning privileges,
Deriving from daily life
Giving gifts

## Punishing Consequences

The parent who saves the child from a potentially disastrous natural consequence should not turn his back on this potential teaching opportunity for the sake of the future safety of the child. By administering a controlled punishing (adverse) consequence such as a spanking sufficient enough to make the child cry, the child learns unconsciously to connect dangerous behavior with pain. The parents then explain to the child why they spanked him and the child repeats this back to the parent. In any behavior that is potentially harmful to the child or others, a punishing consequence will inhibit or at least lessen this behavior.

There are seven categories of Punishing Consequences
Withholding
Withdrawing
Redoing
Reversing the game
Avoiding
Challenging-teasing
Intimidating
*See chart: Types/Examples and Purposes of Just Right Moral Consequences*

<u>*POISE: Individualizing Consequences*</u>

Through POISE, Parent-Observation–Indication-Strategization-Evaluation, parents learn what truly is a punishment or a reward to their child. In this on-going process the parents observe the child's behavioral reactions, the parents note facial expression, body language, voice and verbal indications that allow parents to begin to create an hypothesis of what behaviors are rewards or punishment for their child. The parents then develop strategies to evaluate whether their hypothesis is correct.

Every individual is different. A reward to one is a punishment for another. Spending the day at the beach can be a pleasure to one child and a day of boredom for another. "You were very responsible taking care of your baby sister today, so you can stay up a little later tonight and watch television with your mother and father." The problem is that some children might consider staying up with mom and dad watching television a punishment. In order to know whether a consequence is a reward or punishment, parents must know their child. Many children are manipulative and often confuse the parents by distorting their feelings to avoid punishment. He may state that he "does not want to watch television" when he is truly missing his favorite show.

In other words a parent might notice a child likes to be with a certain set of friends. The parent devises a strategy to invite the child's friends to play in the back yard with his child. This gives the parent the opportunity to evaluate his child's interaction with the group and know his child's tendencies by straightforward observation of the child instead of asking the child. This observational feedback loop of POISE provides quality assurance and confidence to the parents that their interaction with their child is beneficial as they build layer upon layer of understanding of their child.

Often a child does not accurately know what they like or dislike or may be blatantly deceitful to manipulate the parent. The POISE process allows the parent to gain a true picture of what behaviors will be rewards or punishments for the child. By gaining better knowledge of their child's responses to specific consequences, the parents develop more confidence and poise in their interactions with their child.

## *Administering The Just Right Moral Consequence:*

After determining what is a reward or a punishment to a child through the POISE process, the parent has to use the right consequence to shape the child's values, thinking and behavior. In a complex society choosing the right consequence for an individual child requires a systematic approach. Many times the lesson to be learned is not one which is physically threatening, but a moral lesson. In the situation of a moral lesson, the Just Right Moral Consequence approach is used.

Just Right Moral Consequence (JRMC) is an individualized process in judiciously choosing the morally correct and meaningful consequence for a specific child's actions or expressed thoughts in a particular situation. The issue with physical punishment is to stop a harmful behavior to self or others while JRMC is a process to teach a child to develop a moral conscience. The process is both "Just" meaning it judiciously considers all the facts before arriving at a decision and "Right" because the parent, like a competent judge selects the best (right) consequence to make the transgressor learn the moral lesson needed to become a good member of society (family).

**There are Two Steps to Administering a Just Right Moral Consequence.**
• **JUST:** Investigate the behavior or alleged behavior.
• **RIGHT:** Choose the JRMC.

1.    *Investigate the Behavior or Alleged Behavior*

The younger the child usually the less complicated this step. The limits established for a young child are basic and when transgressed are easily noticed. The young child hopefully is under direct supervision of an adult, parent, teacher, caretaker and any transgression would probably be observed by the adult or another child.

The older and more verbal the child, the greater the fact finding phase of being **"Just"** is needed to neutralize the common tendencies of today's American children to be their own defense lawyers. For instance, you inform the child he will go to bed if he hits his sibling again. It is "Just" because you already laid down the law. The parent sees him hit again with his own eyes and the consequence is carried out. If the parent did not see the episode directly then the fact-finding phase becomes necessary. The need to observe and know the behavioral tendencies of your child makes Quantity Time vital in Essential Parenting.

2.    *Choosing the JRMC*

After investigating and learning what actually took place, the parents have to choose a JRMC that will help to enlighten the child as to what is the best choice for a behavior in the next similar situation and why. If the parents learn that the child chose the correct action such as attempting to help her brother, by getting food for him even though she spilled the food, the parent would employ a rewarding consequence and help her clean up the spill. Later she might have a special treat for being such a good girl. If the parent learns she was teasing the younger child, the consequence would match the deed. The selection of the **"Right"** consequence is key to the JRMC

# TYPES/EXAMPLES AND PURPOSES OF JUST RIGHT MORAL CONSEQUENCES

| TYPE | EXAMPLE | PURPOSE |
|------|---------|---------|

## Rewarding Consequences

You have done such a good job you have earned _____.

| TYPE | EXAMPLE | PURPOSE |
|------|---------|---------|
| EARNING PRIVILEGE | Play ball with dad | You did a good job contributing |
| | Go on a trip | so you have earned this |
| | Work on a fun activity | privilege |
| | Watch a movie | |
| | Buy new shoes | |

Earned privilege type consequences motivate the child to make a choice of contributing to others. These are rewarding consequences.

Parents should make use of the many things they give their children in an average day.

| TYPE | EXAMPLE | PURPOSE |
|------|---------|---------|
| DERIVING FROM | Trip to the park | Your family does many wonderful |
| DAILY LIFE | Eating a special meal | things with you for your doing a |
| | Visiting a friend | good job |
| | Going to a restaurant | |

By pointing out the positive aspects of everyday family life, parents will not have to artificially create material consequences.

"You have been a good child and I want to give you _____".

| TYPE | EXAMPLE | PURPOSE |
|------|---------|---------|
| GIVING GIFTS | Take the family car for your date | Your overall positive attitude |
| | Go to a sporting event together | and behavior is appreciated |
| | Play card games or a board game | |
| | Let's go for ice cream | |

This allows the child to realize that his overall attitude and behavior is recognized by his loved ones.

# Punishing Consequences

You can no longer do a certain activity for a certain period of time.

| WITH HOLDING | | |
|---|---|---|
| | Watch television, videos | You have lost the privilege to do |
| | Go to gymnastics, dance, baseball, soccer | (whatever) because you did the |
| | Swim in the pool | misdeed. |
| | Visit friends | |
| | Stay over at friends | |

Withholding is a temporary response to a moderate misbehavior.

This is a more severe consequence than WITHHOLDING for a more severe misbehavior

| WITHDRAWING | | |
|---|---|---|
| | Cold shoulder | "Since you hurt or disappointed us |
| | Removal from team | we will not do this for you." |
| | Sit at table by himself instead of with family | |
| | Stop doing laundry, cooking for child | |
| | Take everything out of child's room | |

Withdrawing is a strong response to a more severe transgression. Calibrated guilt will be produced.

Since you did not do a very good job on _____, you will have to redo it.

| REDOING | | |
|---|---|---|
| | You will redo your homework, rewrite the story | Doing quality work will develop |
| | You will redo the yard work, the mowing | good work habits for the rest of |
| | You will rewash the dishes, the windows | the child's life. |

REDO consequence helps the child to internalize the standards of the parents.

When a child refuses to do something the parent needs to reply that the parent will not allow the child to do the activity.

| REVERSING THE GAME | | |
|---|---|---|
| | You are not allowed to do your chores | "You don't want to do something, |
| | You will go to school in your pajamas because you | now I'm not going to allow you to |
| | did not get up on time | do it." |
| | You cannot eat this food | |

Reverse the game is a power tool that takes the power away from the child and returns it to the parent.

When parents make a judgement that something will be detrimental for the child,

| AVOIDING | AVOIDING the problem is a viable strategy. | |
|---|---|---|
| | Cannot sleep over at _____'s house | I am not comfortable with your |
| | Will not go to that party, dance, game | safety so I cannot allow you to go |
| | Should not see that movie, play, video | there, do that. |

Avoiding a situation minimizes the child's exposure to things that they are not ready to handle.

Teasing has been used throughout history to strengthen certain values and behavior.

| CHALLENGING/TEASING | You cannot help me, you are not strong enough | When you show me you can |
|---|---|---|
| | You cannot find that, you are too young. | handle it, I will allow you to do the |
| | You are too young to memorize multiplication facts. | things you want. |

Teasing is a means of challenging the child to reach certain levels of behavior.

Parents use INTIMIDATION to immediately stop a behavior. (most effective with infants and toddlers)

| INTIMIDATING | Giving the "evil eye" | Used when the behavior must stop |
|---|---|---|
| | Standing over the child showing bigger size | immediately because it can hurt |
| | Raising one's voice | child or others. |
| | Spanking, hitting the child | |

Intimidating a child will inhibit him from hurting himself or others.
An explanation should follow to give the child alternative behaviors in similar situations.

94

process. A list of ten categories of consequences is given at left. Three types of rewarding consequences and seven types of punishing consequences are presented along with examples and purposes:

**There are five guiding principles that are important in arriving at a good choice of a JRMC.**

- POISE, Parent Observation- Indication-Strategization-Evaluation. This process teaches the parents what behaviors are rewards or punishments to their child.

- Least Restrictive Yet Effective Consequence
  A parent should select a low level rather than a high level consequence which gets the desired results. For example, when you tell a child to sit down in a chair for misbehavior and she follows the directions of sitting there until she can tell the parent what she did wrong, nothing more needs to be done. This simple step can be repeated until it is no longer effective.

  The escalation of duration or severity of the consequence should immediately be stopped as soon as the desired result is obtained. The parental knowledge that ratcheting up consequences will eventually work gives parents security in their interaction with their child, preventing frustration that can lead to abuse. By using a measured approach the parents do not deplete their "bag of tricks" and thus have additional consequences, both rewards and punishments, for future child behavior.

- Moderate and Balanced Consequence
  Consequences should remain in the middle of the continuum of possible consequences. Too rewarding or too punitive consequences means a parent is not using the full range and therefore not receiving the full benefit of the consequence. A parent using solely rewarding consequences has to move down the continuum while a parent using solely punishing

95

consequences needs to move up the continuum. The most effective place for a parent is to be in the middle of the continuum. Extremes, too much or too little, are usually abusive.

Since the Industrial Age we defined abuse and neglect in the narrow terms of too much corporal punishment, too much guilt, too high expectations and too little meeting of basic needs. In the Post Industrial Age, it has been taken to the other extreme where too little training, too little guilt, too few expectations, and too much material pampering is the new form of abuse and neglect. Purposeful Discipline realizes that the best results are obtained by remaining in the middle of the disciplinary continuum.

- Incremental Autonomy Through Earning Privileges
  As the child demonstrates more socially commendable behavior, the child ought to receive rewarding consequences called "earning privileges." The younger the child, generally the greater the need for parental control. As the child successfully demonstrates specific competence, the parents are able to reward the child by gradually withdrawing their authority and control providing small doses of adult type behavior. The parent gives the child more legitimate adult choices developing trust in the child until the end of adolescence. The young adult is then responsible for all his own choices making him a viable family and society member. Conversely, if a child's behavior regresses, it is the responsibility of the parent to withhold or even withdraw certain privileges that the child previously enjoyed.

- Examine the Purpose and Type of Consequence

  Parents can readily select an appropriate consequence when the purpose of the consequence and the type of consequence are examined. When the purpose is to reward the child an *Earning Privilege* or a *Deriving from Daily Life* type of consequence can be selected. In order to prevent a possible problem an *Avoiding Consequence* may be used; or *Reversing the Game* a reverse psychology approach can be used. *Withholding* and *Withdrawing* consequences will announce to the child that the parents are displeased while a *Redoing* of the activity focuses on improving the particular behavior. An *Intimidating* consequence inhibits the behavior and a *Challenging/Teasing* consequence motivates the child to try something new.

Too many modern-confused parents have been brainwashed into believing that honesty on the part of the parent will traumatize their child. The reality is that if a child does not begin to understand the possible consequences of his own behavior he will possibly be a threat to himself or others. Not being honest will have a far more negative impact on his future than visualizing the pain his behavior might bring to himself or others. Hopefully the discussion of the purpose of the discipline will inhibit possible future negative behavior while fostering better behavioral choices.

The following charts on the next two pages will give you a visual guide to the steps of Purposeful Discsipline.

# STEPS IN PURPOSEFUL DISCIPLINE

REWARDING APPROPRIATE BEHAVIOR

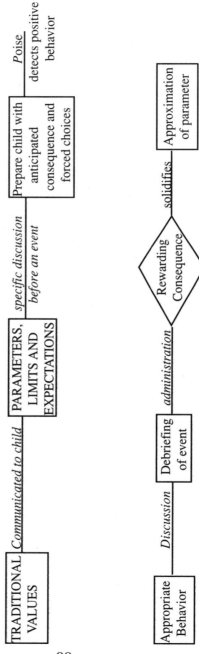

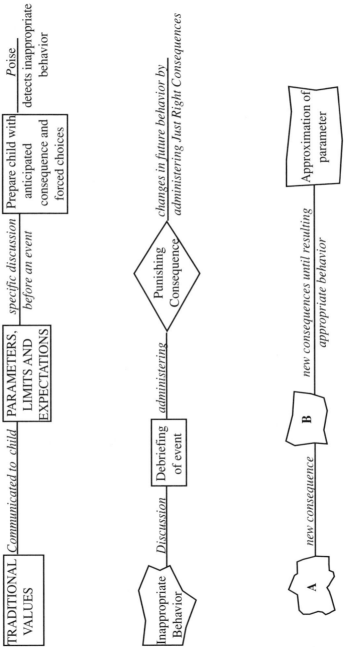

PUNISHING INAPPROPRIATE BEHAVIOR

TRADITIONAL VALUES — *Communicated to child* — PARAMETERS, LIMITS AND EXPECTATIONS — *specific discussion before an event* — Prepare child with anticipated consequence and forced choices — *Poise* detects inappropriate behavior

Inappropriate Behavior — *Discussion* — Debriefing of event — *administering* — Punishing Consequence — *changes in future behavior by administering Just Right Consequences*

**A** — *new consequence* — **B** — *new consequences until resulting appropriate behavior* — Approximation of parameter

99

# DON'T FORGET!!!

The younger the child the more effective are intimidating consequences, such as slapping her hand or behind, giving the evil eye, direct commands, standing over. Therefore use intimidating consequences during infancy and toddler stages. Intimidation is counter-productive when begun in adolescence.

- Instruct by demonstrating correct behavior. Role model.

- Child repeats appropriate behavior until it is done correctly. Redoing until it is done right.

- Always keep your word. If you say it, do it. Consistently follow-up and follow-through. Establish and maintain your credibility as disciplinarian.

- When caught off-guard by a request, say "no" first. This will give you time to reconsider. A "yes" is harder to retract than amending a "no" into a "yes".

- Lowering expectations for a child tends to increase misbehavior while increasing expectations tends to decrease misbehaviors.

- Never give up. Once you start PD look for small changes. This will increase your resolve, patience and prevent you from wearing down.

- Concerned adults (parents) need to remain united on their particular strategies with the child by communicating with each other.

- Avoid situations for which the child is not physically, emotionally or socially prepared.

- When you are reacting to a child out of your needs (anger, frustration) instead of the child's needs- STOP. This is non-productive and may become abusive.

- A child who acts inappropriately is harder to like than a child who acts appropriately.

Purposeful Discipline is in the long run more beneficial to your child's development than any extra curricular activity such as dance class, gymnastics, team sports, karate and so on. Thus, if the child misbehaves, withhold or withdraw her from the activity to make a strong statement, even if you have prepaid for the activity. Your child's development is worth it.

Purposeful Discipline systematic training focuses on core traditional values such as love, reality, honesty, respectfulness, independence, obedience, critical thinking, empathy, conscience, and will power. The Purposeful Discipline training is not the superficial "yes, ma'am", "no sir" that attempts to masquerade as parental training, but is a profound effort to develop the inner character of the child. The Purposefully Disciplined child will possess the inner values that will guide him throughout his life.

# Chapter 5

## Purposeful Discipline
## Systematic Training of the Child

*"Give a man a fish and you feed him for a day. Teach a man to fish and you feed him for a lifetime."*   Chinese Proverb

*"The pupil who is never required to do what he cannot do, never does what he can do."*   John Stuart Mills

Children are not born trained to behave in a culturally correct manner. There is no "instant" two minute microwave training process that will present you with a fully functioning adult. Even with our modern technology, child training is like starting a meal from scratch, a time consuming labor of love with a pinch of this and a dash of that until perfection is achieved.

Cooking a full course meal may take a good portion of a day. Raising an infant to adulthood takes a good portion of a parent's life. Truly it is an on-going commitment that lasts until your last breath. However, the most important and intense part of this commitment is at the start of the child's life. The patterns established from infancy to early adolescence guide children on the right course throughout life.

When a fetus's umbilical cord is cut, the newborn's struggle for life begins. The infant battles to survive while the parents battle to channel the infant's self-centered urges into socially acceptable behavior. If the parents win the initial battles totally and swiftly, the child learns that complying with the parents is the best policy for successful survival. The parents realize if the child follows their experienced parental advice, the child blossoms by quickly learning socially acceptable behavior. Parents who are in charge raise healthy functioning children. On the other hand, confused parents, who allow the child to be in charge, raise unhealthy, dysfunctional children. Life is an adventure with many twists and turns. The parents are responsible for teaching their children how to choose the correct path for themselves through inculcating traditional values.

The "too precious child" syndrome is a parental delusion. Parents who believe their child is the cutest, smartest, prettiest, most creative, the best this or that are setting their offspring up to be neurotic failures. No child can live up to these delusional expectations. No matter how hard the child attempts to compensate, victory is unattainable. Parents are entrusted with their children to prepare them to function independently. A child is not supposed to be a jewel in the parents' crown to show off or impress others. A child is a solemn responsibility as well as a temporary gift, who will, when nurtured and trained properly, mature into a decent, productive, giving, human being.

This nurturing has many forms, from providing basic needs like food, to affection and knowledge for making survival easier and more likely. The common knowledge of life, more traditionally called "common sense", has to be shared by parents with their child. It appears that parents with limited Quantity Time to spend to teach their child common sense has led to common sense becoming quite uncommon. Leaving the windows open on a cold day and complaining about the cold, sleeping less than necessary and wondering why one is tired, not reading lessons thoroughly and insisting there is no answer to the question, eating unhealthy foods while not exercising and complaining about being overweight are all examples of the lack of common sense being taught by parents to their children.

Obviously, it is much easier to raise a child with two reasonable parents: mother and father, with a significant amount of agreement on the importance that each parent's differing perspective brings to their child. Mutual respect between parents is an essential element in maximizing a child's learning to deal with the male and female subcultures that comprise his entire world. When a parent competes with his spouse, the child is the ultimate loser. The child needs both parents working together to train him or her, not one parent putting down the other, confusing the child as to what and who to believe. An inconsistent and garbled message makes training ineffective, often dooming it to failure.

A parent giving material gifts and taking special trips with the child while avoiding confrontation is more concerned with winning a child's favor than developing opportunities for training and genuine intimacy. "Buying them off" does buy parents time to pursue their own needs instead of giving the training the child needs. When a child's needs are not being met, the child attempts to manipulate the adult into giving attention on the child's terms, which often pits one parent against the other. Many squabbling parents think that divorce will end the disagreements, making life better for their children. This rationalization for divorce dismisses two decades of research that has demonstrated the negative impact of this drastic change of status.

The disagreement between parents does not abruptly end with divorce because they will remain connected however distantly by their children. The child will have to learn two family cultures which often involve step-parents and step-siblings. The child will often receive less consistent expectations than before. The child will be placed in positions to play one parent against the other, with limited ability for divorced parents to check with each other on what is happening. The divorced parents will find it difficult to say "no" to the suggestions and demands of the child when they believe the ex-spouse may be maneuvering themselves into a more favorable custody position. Divorce between two normally functioning adults does not simplify, but usually complicates the training of a child, and does not minimize but maximizes the potential for a child to manipulate his divorced parents.

Children attempt to meet their own immediate gratification without understanding long term consequences. They do this through crying, throwing tantrums, passive-aggressive non-talking, affection giving or withholding, refusing to comply or playing shy. The parent counters the child's tendency for immediate gratification through establishing precise and clearly understood standards and expectations as well as consistent consequences for those standards and expectations. The self-centered child wants what she wants and the experienced parents give the child what they believe will help her be successful in her future, not what the child may want at a given moment. Obvious to the adults, and not so obvious to the child, is the necessity of delaying immediate gratification for success in a civilized world.

It is common knowledge that boys who grow up without their fathers are twice as likely to end up in prison than are boys who grow up with their fathers. When a single, unmarried or divorced mother raises a girl she is more likely to experience teen pregnancy. Teenagers coming from single parent homes or stepparent homes are more likely to possess drugs, own a weapon, or assault someone at school than teens from intact families. Also significant is the well known fact that young children living with both biological parents are at a much lower risk of physical or sexual abuse than children in other living arrangements. The alternative lifestyle proponents cannot rationally dismiss the overwhelming evidence to support the importance of both a mother and a father providing input in the training of their child. A child benefits from the role modeling of the behaviors expected for both male and female subcultures and direct training of specific skills and behaviors for optimal functioning in a society.

A single parent needs to compensate for the lack of a mate by making a conscious decision to include a substitute father or mother figure in the child's life. The substitute can be a grandparent, sibling, or friend as long as the involvement of the individual is consistent and the individual models appropriate gender behavior. It is difficult to raise a child with two functioning parents, and is an even greater task for a single parent. It can be done and has been done with concentrated effort and continual support from significant others.

Research has demonstrated that training starts as early as in the prenatal stage. The expectant mother's activities consciously or unconsciously have a direct impact on the developing child. Exposure of an unborn child to a particular diet, certain music, drugs or alcohol abuse has been shown to affect the child's emotions and behavior as a newborn. The mother's behavior directly and the father's behavior indirectly have an immediate influence on a fetus. Thus, by their status, parents are granted immense potential to shape and influence the mental, emotional, physical, and spiritual aspects of their child. This means when parents have a clear and consistent vision of the type of child they want and are willing to put forth the effort, an effective training program will start to emerge.

The baby screaming, spitting out food, biting of the mother's breast when nursing, pulling the cat's fur, holding out hands to be picked up will be responded to by the parent in a coherent, well considered, effective manner or in an inconsistent and random

106

manner. We as parents have a finite time for our intensive training, traditionally eighteen years. The earlier and more well thought-out our strategies, the closer the vision of our child will align with reality.

These strategies are based on the observable behavior of the child not on some preconceived, artificial agenda or labeling of a child. Each child is as distinctive as a snowflake or an ocean wave. A child comes with genetically determined predispositions that make it ridiculous to attempt to approach each child in the same manner. The child's observable behavior will be the determining factor in formulating specific strategies and the intensity or duration of any one approach. A strong willed aggressive child will probably require a more intensive time of training to teach obedience while a withdrawn, fearful child will probably have more difficulty in learning certain aspects of dealing with the real world. The training intensity and duration of each aspect discussed in this book will be determined by the child's internal timetable.

*NOTE: The child's reaction to the training described in this chapter should ultimately direct the parents' specific application of these techniques to gain the desired behavioral results. The POISE (Parental Observation-Indication-Strategization-Evaluation) process, defined in the introduction and elaborated in Chapter 4, provides the necessary feedback to determine if the parents' particular intervention or training with the child is effective or not.*

The following training is a practical list, but is by no means an exhaustive list. As one begins to train a child in these areas other possibilities will become apparent fitting the needs of the particular child and/or family unit. Love, obedience, "the wrap," independence, critical thinking, potty training, respectfulness, honesty, reality, conscience, empathy, pain, will power, and creativity development are specifically discussed. It should be recognized from the beginning that the earlier a parent starts to train the child, the easier and better flow from one area to another will take place. The external training of the child by the parent will be culminated when the child is consistently disciplined reactively as daily problems arise or proactively through a well thought out training program and the child clearly demonstrates an internalizing of the teachings and training.

The modern-confused parent waits until the child is approaching or actually reaches adolescence before attempting to start training the child, and then starts usually out of frustration. It becomes apparent through reading this chapter that the modern-confused parent's approach is irrational. Giving carte blanche freedom of choice to a child with limited experience and then attempting to assert parental power during adolescence is a formula for frustration, hostility, and rebellion. Essential Parenting™ uses Purposeful Discipline to maximize authority early and, as the child succeeds, the parents withdraw allowing their child gradual autonomy: a rational formula for success.

## LOVING TRAINING

*"Little children are still the symbol of the eternal marriage between love and duty." George Eliot*

Loving a child requires parents to do many things for the sake of the child. A father working two jobs is demonstrating love for his family. A pregnant mother being concerned with her diet, exercise, stress level, sleeping pattern, use of medication for the sake of her unborn child is beginning the "Loving Training". After birth, holding, kissing, caressing, smiling at, spending time, and playing games with the child establishes the foundation of the bond of love between mother and child. The father's feeling of satisfaction as he observes his wife feeding their baby and the mother's feeling of pride and happiness as she observes the father playing with their child is part of establishing the bond that brings and holds the family together. Parents should be at a place in their lives where they are ready and grateful to be given the opportunity to nurture a child and not be resentful of the child. In short, they need to be emotionally mature.

The selection by the parents of certain spontaneous behaviors of the child for acknowledgment and approval continue to deepen the loving connection between child and parent. Obviously the more time the parents are with the child, the greater the opportunity for all types of training

## LOVING TRAINING

| ESSENTIAL PARENTING™ | MODERN-CONFUSED PARENTING |
|---|---|
| Increases Quantity Time opportunities to seize the positive moment. | Thinks quality time will compensate for not being there. |
| Knows child-rearing requires time for training. | Believes quality time can make up for parental absence |
| Relishes and knows parental role. | Fluctuates in parental role from idolizing to frustration. |

The modern-confused parent has been led to believe that the child will automatically conform to cultural behavioral patterns. Therefore, the modern-confused parents have little responsibility in the area of training and spend the majority of their time entertaining the child. Eventually this vision of being a playmate and friend is shattered by the self-centered, acting-out behavior of the child, leaving the parent in a state of confusion and frustration. Essential Parenting™ through Purposeful Discipline believes that knowledge needs to be transferred to the child to insure the success of the child's future. As the Essential Parenting™ trained parents are immersed in Loving Training; the parents naturally realize the importance of the next stage of training, obedience training, in order to insure the well being of their child.

# OBEDIENCE TRAINING

*"Obedience is in a way the mother of all virtues."* St. Augustine

*"Let the child's first lesson be obedience and the second will be what thou wilt."*    Benjamin Franklin

Since healthy parents love their children, protecting them is a natural manifestation of that love.   Instructions such as, " do not run in the parking lot", "don't touch the stove", "stop teasing the dog," have to be enforced immediately or the child may be seriously or even fatally injured.  The words "**STOP**" and "**NO**," if religiously followed by the child, will extend the protective arm of the parent.  There is no need or time for negotiation.  The parent commands and the child responds.  Obedience to a parent when the child is young increases the efficiency of all training.  A child, who listens to his parents and follows their instructions explicitly, streamlines the training process and lessens the environment for frustration.

Modern-confused parents are under the misconception that an obedient child will become a rigid, blindly obedient adult.  The opposite is true.  A well loved, obedient child who successfully completes tasks develops self-competency.  A child who feels self-competent is more likely to have the inner strength and security to appropriately question authority.  On the other hand, the overtly disobedient child will have, at best, limited opportunity to casually interact with authority figures.  The disobedient adolescent who exhibits obnoxious behavior repulses even his own "unconditionally loving" parents.  As the respectful, obedient child reaches adolescence, it is natural for her to begin to assert her independence.  In this process of preparing to leave the nuclear family the teenager will challenge her parents in her quest to "leave the nest".  This challenging of parental authority by a formerly obedient teenager is a healthy sign of her disengagement from her immediate family.

An obedient younger child accepts the superior power of the parent. A disobedient child challenges at every turn the superior power of the parent. A non compliant soldier quickly learns the power of the chain of command or suffers the brig or even discharge. Soldiers in boot camp are put into situations where their emotions are telling them to yell back but their brains are telling them they had better listen. The armed forces learned long ago that one disobedient member endangers everyone. The parent, like the drill sergeant, needs to begin training with simple commands and work up to more complex ones. The initial commands like "stop" and "no" must be said in a firm voice.

The earlier the training begins the more rapid the results. A one or two year old child has few resources to disregard his towering, all powerful parents unless his parents are ignorant of the importance or unwilling to put forth the effort necessary at this stage of child rearing to begin obedience training. Once the parent establishes the pattern of obedience it is difficult to reverse. The child's natural inclination to please the parent and the parent's love for the child makes for easy sailing on this obedience course.

Parental absenteeism, discord between parents, divorce, mental illness, and most important, ignorance, destroy the conditions necessary for almost effortless, natural obedience training. A child who displays tantrums indicates a lack of, or a poor attempt at, obedience training. Eradicating tantrums takes more effort than if one began obedience training early in a consistently loving manner. A tantrum means a child believes she has as much or more power than a parent. When a parent capitulates to a child and allows the child to do or get what she is demanding, the parents are unwittingly feeding into the intensity and duration of the tantrum.

Ignoring a tantrum as long as the child does not obtain what she is demanding will diminish, in the long run, the child's use of this strategy. The child will realize that tantrum behavior does not pay and her parents are truly in power in her life. The problem with ignoring tantrum behavior is that it takes time and almost super human discipline on the part of the parent not to react. Often parents take the easy way out and give in to the demands of the child. This confuses her into thinking tantrums indeed do work or they spank the child too softly to get the child's attention or too violently to allow the child to understand that she has the problem, not the parent.

## OBEDIENCE TRAINING

| ESSENTIAL PARENTING™ | MODERN-CONFUSED PARENTING |
|---|---|
| Teaches commands like "no" and "stop" in infancy by giving an adverse stimulus like slapping hand, time out, taking away toy | Thinks a child should not be trained like a dog, not listening is normal for children. |
| Explains to the child the negative results of the misbehavior and positive long term results of acceptable behavior. | Misses the opportunity to teach child by ignoring misdeed. |
| Asks the child to tell the misdeed or tells it to the child and has the child repeat. | Makes excuses for the child's transgression |
| Wins every confrontation with the child | Wins some and loses some giving the child the message he can win if he battles hard enough. |
| Thinks child should have a healthy fear of the parent's power | Thinks parents should be the child's friend. |
| Establishes the habit of obedience allowing for greater appreciation of child | Thinks disobedience is a sign of a strong independent thinker |

The modern-confused parent appears to believe that a child needs to express himself as soon as possible to become a strong and independent adult. This translates into a child getting whatever he wants whenever he wants it. Disobedience is viewed as a child demonstrating his independent thinking. This confused parents' perception of their strong, independent thinking child collapses

112

when the child departs the parental protective umbrella. Adults outside the parents' influence, such as teachers, doctors, parents of childhood friends, or law enforcement officers who have exposure to children, will view this as spoiled and disruptive behavior. The confused parent will be forced to ignore other authority figures or, if healthy, begin to re-evaluate their premises and approach to child rearing.

If the child throws tantrums and is unwilling to listen to simple and reasonable commands then "The Wrap" may be the most effective means of getting the child back on track.

# THE "WRAP"-

## Re-establishing Power, Eliminating Tantrums

An efficient and rapid method of eliminating a tantrum is a direct battle with the child to establish or re-establish the obvious reality that the parent possesses more power. The initial battle may be intense and last up to forty-five minutes to an hour, but each successive battle will be less intensive and shorter in duration.

The "Loving Wrap" is a decisive method of establishing one's power with an unruly child. How is it done? The adult sits the child on her lap with the adult's arms firmly wrapped around the child, but not so the child is being squeezed. The adult wraps her legs over the child's legs to keep from being kicked. The child needs to be positioned a little to the side so the child cannot fling his head back into the adult's chin.

USING THE "WRAP" TECHNIQUE

For use with child small enough to be easily restrained; age 2-8

The parent speaks calmly to the child and politely asks him to do a simple command like "sit in the chair". The child will probably resist and refuse to do as asked.

1. The parent puts the child in the chair. The child refuses to comply by being defiant.

2. The parent sits in the chair and puts the child on his lap telling him he must sit in the chair, which is now the parent's lap. If the child starts to struggle, the parent uses the "wrap" technique- folding his arms over the child's chest and crossing one or both legs over the child's legs, position the child a little to one side so he cannot fling back his head and hit the parent's chin.

3. The struggle will ebb and renew until the child is exhausted. The parent asks the child if he is ready to sit in the chair. The child may say a defiant "no" and begins flailing all over again while the parent remains calmly holding the child tightly in "the wrap". When the child stops flailing the parent relaxes his grip to correspond to the child's gaining control over his tantrum. It may take several tries of letting the child sit in the chair and then returning to the "wrap" before the child is tired and relents. At no time should the parent raise his/her voice or demonstrate any anger.

4. The parent can relax the hold and let the child sit in the chair by himself as originally commanded to do. Once the child does this correctly, the parent has won and this battle is over. The child realizes he is powerless to win and accepts defeat by following what the parent asked.

5. Right after this initial victory the parent gives another simple command like "hug me" or "shake my hand" and the obedience pattern has begun.

6. Any small misbehavior needs to be confronted, a command used and the child needs to comply or reuse the "wrap".

The previously disobedient child starts to realize the overwhelming power of the parents and realizes his needs will be better met by joining rather than fighting the parents. There will be other attempts at testing parental limits, but a firm parental response will settle the issue without a full-blown tantrum. When a child learns that the parent has the power to hand out consequences and the will to follow through on those consequences, the child has no other viable recourse than to become an obedient child.

An obedient child's spirit is not crushed. Instead, complying removes the need to uselessly and destructively expend energy and time challenging parental authority and frees up energy to develop the uniqueness of the child's personality. Obedience allows the child and parent to spend more stress free time together which encourages more loving reactions between parent and child. Instead of resentful battling, parent and child share their time and space in peaceful harmony. The power of the parent is undeniable and peaceful coexistence becomes the norm in this well functioning home.

A functioning family has little need for "drill sergeant" commands. Children in functioning families want to please parents and parents are adequately relaxed to make polite requests that are reasonably completed. An obedient and reasonable child is an easy child to live with and train to meet the milestones of life. One of the milestones of childhood in becoming independent is potty training. The parent should not wait for this process to just happen. Through observation in <u>Essential Parenting</u>™, the parent knows when the child is physiologically ready and breaks down the task for the child to complete the training in a reasonable length of time.

# POTTY TRAINING

*"Help me do it myself."  Maria Montessori*

The current medical and psychological view for toilet training expectations is summed up in the catch phrase "the child will let you know when he is ready".  Parents are lulled into thinking the child will announce that he is self-trained.  Dr. Barry Brazleton, M.D. has proclaimed on a Pampers commercial that Pampers are improved and larger, to remove the concern of toilet training.  It is for these reasons that many parents have not even begun toilet training when their child has already reached the ripe old age of four years!  However the completion of toilet training usually is a pre-requisite for entering an academic preschool program. So there still are some age appropriate benchmarks existent for children.

A child can use defecation as a weapon to punish or manipulate the parent.  A child who has learned how to go to the bathroom in a civilized manner is one step closer to being a healthy and competent person. When the child completes another milestone like toilet training, he is naturally encouraged to attempt other new behaviors in his quest to become a viable independent individual. Today's pendulum has swung so far to the other extreme that it has obliterated child rearing expectations to remove any possibility of stigma from children who were unable to meet this expectation.  In the process these experts have taken away the benchmarks that directed parents down the road of child rearing.

116

# POTTY TRAINING

| ESSENTIAL PARENTING™ | MODERN-CONFUSED PARENTING |
|---|---|
| Expects to complete training by 18 months to 2 years | Waits until the child is ready |
| Commits to finishing once started | Has inconsistent follow-up, fits and jerks |
| Continues despite obstacles | Allows obstacles to interrupt training |
| Firmly reprimands child's regressions | Sees regressions as reasons to suspend training until child is ready. |

Historically potty training was seen as important to complete as soon as possible for sanitary reasons as well as relieving parents of the burden of an untrained child. However, Sigmund Freud's writing of "anal retention" has swung the pendulum to the other extreme of no potty training to eliminate any trauma to the child. The modern day trauma, however, is that children are being seen as if they were mentally retarded or emotionally disturbed because they are not potty trained at the traditionally expected age.

The confused parent waits until the child is "ready" to avoid being guilty of traumatizing the child. Being "ready" really means when the child decides to train himself or the parent becomes sufficiently embarrassed, due to the age of the child, to finally motivate the child to use the toilet. The confused parent may start at an earlier age using training pants on their child but changes back to diapers when going out or whenever inconvenient to train the child. An illness, move, trip, or other circumstance usually will delay or suspend this inconsistent process. The modern-confused parent has no strong commitment to potty training the child.

The Essential Parenting™ trained parent knows that the process once started needs to be completed successfully at about eighteen months of age. The parent sees signs from the child that the child is physically and emotionally ready for the process. The Essential

117

Parented™ child, already obedient, follows the instructions to wear the training pants and to sit on the toilet at certain intervals until the association is made between the urgency feeling of needing to eliminate and sitting on the toilet. As with any other disciplinary situation, when the child tests the parent by not following the process, the Essential Parenting™ trained parent will firmly reprimand the child to re-establish the potty training rules until completion.

A physically healthy child attempts from birth to do things on his own. Moving the eyes, lifting the head, rolling over, and becoming toilet trained are early attempts by the child to exert his physical power to become an independent individual. The skills necessary for social independence are more easily taught to an obedient rather than a disobedient child. In fact, many youngsters' battles fought over independence can be avoided if the child joins the parents rather than opposes them.

## INDEPENDENCE TRAINING

*"If you think you can, you can and if you think you can't, you are right." American Traditional*

It is a parent's responsibility to help a child become independent. An infant naturally attempts to do things on its own: beginning with the babbling sounds, then picking up the head, and trying to grab objects. The infant attempts to explore and manage his environment. A healthy parent will encourage and assist the child's natural urge to become an independent human being. A loved and obedient child who is striving for independence is a wonderful candidate for independence training. The loved and obedient child will try to more actively repeat the sound of the word that her parents have modeled and will more readily imitate the parent, demonstrating how to pick up her pants or urinate in the toilet.

Obviously the independence training should go from the simple to the more complex: from simple behavior to more complex behavior, from simple ideas to more complex ideas. The parent observes the child and assists her progress in order to complete successfully a particular independence goal. Through observing the child's behavior and skill level, parents may feel that reaching a significant milestone is imminent. Once the parents' expectations are in place and the parents substantiate the child's physical readiness, the parents can channel and encourage the child's accomplishing the training goal.

This may take the form of dicing food into safe small pieces in order for the child to feed herself by hand, then moving on to using a fork or spoon to pick up child sized pieces of bread, and at last using a dull knife to cut vegetables. The same process of starting with a simple activity and then moving on to a more complex activity should be used with all activities that will help the child become independent. Zippering or buttoning activities will move from objects easy for a young child to handle to more difficult pieces of clothing.

As the child matures the parents will want to introduce their child to yard work, painting, and building which again requires the parent breaking down the task into simple steps. In addition, folding laundry, cutting vegetables, washing dishes, setting the table, mashing potatoes, making sandwiches or other household tasks teach elementary independence skills. The parents place responsibility on themselves to create new ways to teach these skills displaying patience and encouragement while never ridiculing or being sarcastic. Developing self-competency in children is a powerful way to insure a child's feelings of self worth. This increase in self worth derived from self-competency strengthens a child's natural inclination to question and create new ideas and thoughts.

# INDEPENDENCE TRAINING

| ESSENTIAL PARENTING™ | MODERN-CONFUSED PARENTING |
|---|---|
| Encourages child to begin doing things for herself as soon as possible, dressing, feeding, potty | Continues to do for the child |
| Breaks down more difficult tasks into manageable parts for child | Says, "That is too hard for you," keeping the child a baby |
| Shows child how to do new things without sarcasm or ridicule | It is easier to do it myself. |
| Encourages child to experiment and ask questions to do things better | Does not trust child to experiment or think on his own |
| Expects adolescent to become more financially responsible; and independent by buying own car, paying for college | Parents keep child dependent by paying for everything |

The modern-confused parent vacillates from allowing the child to do whatever the child wants, to doing it for the child. This is a hit and miss process depending on the mood of the parent. If the child pulls something off a shelf and breaks it the parent could chalk it up to the "terrible twos", yell at the child, "child proof" the home or immediately hand the child what he wants before the child breaks it. There is no preparation of the environment to establish training possibilities and no thought of breaking skills down to simple steps and then encouraging the child to complete the activity. Essential Parenting™ not only prepares the environment to establish training possibilities for independent action, but also for independent thought. The modern-confused parents pay for material things to encourage dependence and insure being liked by the child. The EP parent expects children to purchase significant items such as a car and college education to increase his appreciation and motivation for these things. EP assists the child in developing his critical thinking abilities by providing a strong tradition of values, thought and belief system for the child to build upon in order to function in a highly complex, sophisticated and often deceitful society.

# CRITICAL THINKING TRAINING

*"I think therefore I am."   Rene' Descartes*

The ability for an individual to be able to critically think has never been more important than it is today. The sophistication of politicians, salespeople, media personnel, and others to consciously distort the truth for their own personal advancement has reached a level that only the most discerning individuals will be able to detect. Methodically "spin doctors" use doctored photographs, music, "docudramas", and expert testimony as some of their tools to alter the perceptions of masses of people regardless of how powerful the reality of the event. Even Hitler's propaganda machine pales in comparison to the level of present day manipulation of the truth.

The permissive/material child rearing approach proclaims their procedures develop a thinking child though reality appears to indicate otherwise. The permissive/material belief system is predicated on allowing the child to say and do what the child wants. By parents restraining from imposing their values, beliefs and morals on the child, the child will be free to independently develop his own improved version of dealing with the world. Parents are supposed to ignore inappropriate behavior, appease the child in power struggles and reinforce their "cute" primitive thinking without attempting to extend or correct their thinking.

Imposing the parent's thinking on the child is a "no, no" as it will impede the child from developing his unique thinking style. Children are encouraged to think of themselves as equal to the parents even though the child knows on some level that he lacks the life experience of his parents. A child who feels equal or superior to her parent's thinking ability will naturally tend to exhibit more disrespectful behavior than a child who is taught by the parents to understand the breadth of experience of the older and wiser parent.

Placing the "too precious child" on a pedestal is supposed to create an emotionally strong, independent thinker who will be successful in life. The obtaining of a "black belt" in karate is supposed to insure physical toughness, participating in gymnastics class- a shot at the Olympics while taking tennis lessons- future professional stardom. Parents expend enormous amounts of energy, time, and money on chasing their dream for their child. Only later do they realize that their child has grown tired of the hard work and discipline necessary to reach the parent's goal. The child has become disillusioned with the world outside of the protective arm of the parents. Often the child is psychologically devastated, regressing into more babied behavior or angrily demanding adult freedom without the accompanying responsibility.

The unrealistic parental expectations for the child, without the necessary preparation, leave the child in an unappreciative and disagreeable mood. The parents pretend that their child's behavior does not bother them, since it is only a phase. However, the parents distance themselves from the child by eating, visiting, and entertaining themselves separately from their children. This distancing and rebelling phenomenon between child and parents usually seen in adolescent years has been declared as normal by the permissive/material proponents in order to mask the failure of this child rearing approach. The child's thinking is not accomplished by critically analyzing things, but by doing the opposite, simply by rebelling at the expectations of parents, teachers, and other authority figures. A child in rebellion is in emotional conflict, reacting against authority not critically analyzing in order to find the socially appropriate solutions to his particular dilemma.

# CRITICAL THINKING TRAINING

| ESSENTIAL PARENTING™ | MODERN-CONFUSED PARENTING |
|---|---|
| Establish firm beliefs, values and moral system | Does not want to impose values, morals, and beliefs |
| Teach obedience to insure the child's ability to listen to adult's suggestions, advice and direction | Ignores and appeases child's misbehavior and thinking (preciously cute) |
| Spend Quantity Time together eating dinner together and discussing each family members daily events | Spends only "quality time" together, often eats separately from family and frequently allows overnights at friends |
| Participates with children in analyzing news, television shows, newspaper articles, and books. Discusses issues, events challenging child's comprehension and thinking. | Allows child to have separate television set and be isolated watching it. Parent makes the child think his superficial views are valid and profound. (He is so bright.) |
| Explains to child the long-term benefits of particular valued behaviors. | Ignores child's behavior without comment. |
| Gives child projects to complete on her own as weeding, cooking, and cleaning. | Takes child to extra curricular activities like karate, dance, and gymnastics. |
| Expects child to solve own problems as much as possible and allows child to learn from failure. | Bails child out of problems by becoming involved and solving them for the child. |
| Encourages child to respectfully listen to adult conversation and answer questions afterwards. | Allows child to interact with adults as an equal bragging about how "special" the child is. |
| Take visits to friends or relatives and afterwards discusses issues,, ideas and behaviors, which were observed. | Make visits without the child. |
| Take trips and discuss historic sites, museums and culturally different experiences. | Take trips to entertainment attractions as Disney, Universal Studios and shopping malls. |
| As the child's thinking matures he is given more decision-making ability. | Child is included in decision making as an equal from early age. |
| Make child aware through discussion and teasing that his thinking is less mature and valid than his parent's. | Listens to the child and pretends that what they say is reasonable. |

| As the child socially matures and earns privileges, he is given incremental freedom and responsibility to make choices and decisions as long as they meet parental expectations. | As the child chronologically matures, child fluctuates from demanding to be treated as an adult to being treated as a child. Wants total freedom now without any responsibility for own actions. |
| --- | --- |

In Essential Parenting™, the child is given a time tested and traditional value system by the parent to compare and contrast with other approaches to life. The child is provided with on-going concrete training in EP to evaluate his thinking strategies. By incrementally increasing freedom with corresponding responsibilities which the child has earned, a child gradually embellishes his core traditional values, thinking, and beliefs. He may also temporarily or permanently alter them. At least with open and respectful discussions with his parents, the EP trained child has an opportunity to critically examine aspects of a comprehensive traditional value system, without blindly rejecting all of the traditional values, thinking, and belief system. The rejection of all traditional values leaves the child in a void where he is vulnerable to accepting a destructive or inferior value system without critical thought, just to address the basic need of belonging.

Critical thinking is an evolving process that has to begin with a strong foundation of values, thinking, and belief system. The permissive/materialistic proponents encourage the child to develop this ability practically on her own, while Essential Parenting™ provides guidelines to assist the parent in helping the child develop critical thinking abilities. EP does not leave critical thinking to chance. EP uses a systematic approach to train a child to gain the skills and abilities in critical thinking. It takes parental courage to be responsible for determining the training agenda for one's child. EP trained parents, like any parents, want their child to like them, but their first priority is to do the things necessary to enhance their child's potential for a healthy life. Teaching respectfulness is a social skill that increases social acceptance. Respectfulness Training has practically vanished from our cultural expectations because parents are fearful of their child not liking them when they tell the child what to do.

## RESPECTFULNESS TRAINING

*"Civility costs nothing and buys everything."*  *Lady Mary Wortley Montagu*

A child who respects others gains the respect of others. A parent who trains a child to be respectful gives the child the advantage of being accepted by others throughout his life. A child does not have a gene that programs her to be respectful. A responsible adult has to role model as well as to give energy and knowledge instructing the child on what constitutes respectful behavior. A human infant has limited ability for its own survival and has to rely on the parent for almost everything. The infant begins life by necessity in a self-centered posture. The parent, by providing food, shelter, and safety, has all the levers of power to bring the infant from a totally dependent state to a more autonomous state. The parent must spend time interacting with the infant for the child to become a more social individual. Through thoughtful adult interaction with the infant, the child will move from self-centeredness to consideration for others.

# RESPECTFULNESS TRAINING

| ESSENTIAL PARENTING™ | MODERN-CONFUSED PARENTING |
|---|---|
| Role models respectful behavior and demands it in return | Role models being an equal to child with few or no demands |
| Teaches proper behavior and manners please, thank you, table manners | Accepts child's behavior as cute without direct training or correction |
| Teaches children to listen to authority figures | Allows children to ignore or be silly with adults |
| Allows only respectful peers in the child's life | Is tolerant of peer's inappropriate behavior |
| Teaches children to be cooperative and pitch in whenever possible | Does things for the child without requiring their cooperation |
| Requires child to respect rights of others, good sportsmanship | Makes excuses for child's harm to others |
| Expects child to act her age | Allows child to act silly |
| Pushes child to do his best | Allows child to get by |
| Enforces child following rules by demanding more from own child than others | Disregards rules and allows child to take advantage of others |

Treating a child respectfully is a powerful means of teaching respect. "Role Modeling" often takes place unconsciously, although it is the foundation for respectfulness training. As the child matures, the parent continues to role model respectful behavior when opportunities occur to teach manners, appreciation for the feelings of others, and being truthful. Role modeling is an important part but not the total answer to teaching values. Essential Parenting™ requires the child to perform certain specific behaviors such as sitting properly, saying "please" and "thank you", using eating utensils correctly, and so on. The Essential Parenting™ trained parents require the child to listen to authority figures, censor their child's friends, expect their child to act her age, follow rules, and help out others with purpose and consistency that will produce a responsible and respectful person.

126

The confused parent does not have the expectation or committed purpose of producing a respectful child and therefore will not develop a respectful child. Making an excuse for misdeeds by calling them "cute", blaming them on "the stage he is going through", or saying she is being silly, will eventually short change the child by being socially ill-prepared. Modern confused parents allow their child to make negative choices such as not "pitching in" with the rest of the family, associating with negative peers, and not following the rules of the house without having consequences. They appear not to be aware that these choices will produce an ungrateful, immature, and disrespectful child.

The confused parents are under the false assumption that their child can raise herself through making her own choices, thus eliminating the possibility of the confused parents later being blamed for traumatizing their child. The fact is a youngster does not have the experience base to make good choices and therefore will diffuse her energy going off on tangents and testing limits. The child of a confused parent, not being trained to be respectful, will be more likely to turn against her parents than a child receiving directed positive training that works.

Training a child to be honest takes direct intervention. It is rare if not impossible for a child to develop this value on his own and it is not uncommon for an individual to take the path of least resistance, the easy way, by lying to get what he wants. It is uncommon, but honorable for an individual to be honest. It is also in their best interest on their long journey through life.

# HONESTY TRAINING

*"The truth shall set you free." John 8:23*

*"Honesty is the best policy." Miguel de Cervantes*

Being popular can most easily be obtained by giving others
something for nothing or telling someone what they want to hear.
In essence politicians and salespersons have successfully practiced
the art of being subtle liars. Politicians say one thing in one
community and the exact opposite in front of the next audience.
The television flashes dark haired men and a voice says " natural,
real color" and then goes on to try and sell a hair dye that is
unnatural and unreal.

In the United States, honor students have a high incidence of
cheating and the most popular students are often the best liars. On
the surface the phoniness, cheating, and lying of politicians, sales
people, and high achieving students is the road to follow. In the
long run, this road is treacherously filled with potential disasters.
Eventually constituents, customers, and loved ones uncover the
truth, becoming disappointed and shocked. Most importantly the
individual attempting to live the lies has to face up to the
shallowness of his existence.

An individual who is honest with himself and others will be
mentally healthy, trustworthy, and more likely to reach
relationship and spiritual goals in life. Telling the truth keeps an
individual on course. The problem with Honesty Training is that it
requires a long-term commitment by parents to spend Quantity
Time with their child. There is no short cut to insure the positive
result of honesty. It requires a constant vigil of the child's
behavior to correct any deviation from the truth. Lying is
powerful because it gets short-term dividends, making it readily
habit forming. The better the liar, the more the reward and the

more difficult to train to be honest. It is for this reason "nipping it in the bud" is the most effective approach in the initial stage of lying.

"My child does not lie" -said by a parent can only happen in a society of small families and parents who spend limited time with their children. In the past when a child lied in a large family, the other children would tell the parents. Parents would be directed by circumstances to determine who was telling the truth. It became a tedious job for parents, but was necessary to keep peace in the family. With the advent of both parents working, small families, and rampant divorce, parents have become more playmates and less authority figures inculcating values.

Telling the truth is low on the priority list of valued behaviors of the modern-confused parent. The reasoning of the modern confused parent is if their child likes the parent, the child is more likely to have a high self-concept. This is often true, in the short run, as long as the parents are there to protect the child's feelings. As soon as the parents are no longer able to run interference, the child's cute, manipulative distortions of the truth will begin to become a problem for other authority figures in the child's life. The confused parents sacrifice their child's understanding of reality by artificially bolstering the child's self-concept even when the parent knows the child is not accurate or is pretending to be what he is not. This confuses the child and does not allow him to begin to learn how to distinguish between reality and fantasy.

A young child has limited understanding of reality and fantasy. The child needs to be taught by the parent what is reality and what is fantasy. The Essential Parenting™ parent honestly points out to the child instances in life that demonstrate the distinction between reality and fantasy. They expose their children to diverse community experiences. A trip to a nursing home, urban center, ghetto, farmers market, upscale development, college campus, or dairy farm can be shared experiences to build upon in distinguishing between reality and fantasy. When EP parents and children are viewing the media, the parent acts as an active guide assisting the child in this process. The parents honest sharing of their appraisal of a staged event like professional wrestling, a cartoon, and movie special effects, is necessary for the child to get a clear understanding of the world around him. An older child not knowing the distinction between reality and fantasy is at a disadvantage. Lying is not fantasy. Lying is being aware of the truth and saying the opposite.

## HONESTY TRAINING

| ESSENTIAL PARENTING™ | MODERN-CONFUSED PARENTING |
|---|---|
| Role models the truth | Believes truth is relative |
| Understands telling the truth has to be taught | Believes a child naturally tells the truth or all children lie |
| Concern for child being addicted to lying | Concern for child's self concept in questioning child, parent unwilling to admit incompetence |
| Places a priority on truth | Places priority on material things and social acceptance of child |
| Teaches lessons on immorality lying and benefits of truth | Confused about the importance, everyone lies |
| Observes, actively investigates, and resolves any situation where child may have lied | Covers for the child's lies to avoid embarrassment to child and especially to parent |
| Positive consequences for truth | Denies: my child doesn't lie, no need for consequences |
| Zero tolerance for lying | Lies are inevitable and acceptable. |

Honesty training requires a strong personal commitment of the parents to monitor themselves to be truthful and then to closely monitor their child. There is no short cut to Honesty Training. The Essential Parenting™ trained parent is like radar scanning the child's horizons for signs of dishonesty. The EP trained parent understands that we are under a constant barrage of lies through advertising, politics, media, and sadly by the average person. Thus the development of an honest child requires personal motivation to sit down with one's child and teach moral lessons learned in the parent's life through personal heroes and the use of historic moral stories. Being intolerant of lying in a time period of great tolerance for negative actions requires strong personal conviction.

The cultural relativists have destroyed the pillars of truth by dismissing the possibility that individuals can raise children above the commonplace lying. The pronouncement that everybody lies, the tearing down of our great leaders, and encouraging children to exaggerate and tell "white lies," are the tools the cultural relativists have used to undermine the standards of raising an exemplary, honorable, truthful individual. No matter how hard the cultural relativists try, however, they cannot eliminate what is real. Reality has been here in our past, is here in the present, and will be here in the future. Reality Training helps a child to live life more fully with more understanding.

## REALITY TRAINING

*"If there is no struggle, there is no progress."* Fredrick Douglas

Reality is that in nature, which actually exists: fact or truth. Fantasy, on the other hand, exists in the imagination, an illusory mental image, not real. Parents have the responsibility to train and teach reality to their children to help insure their survival in a dangerous world. Running in front of a car, sticking a key into an electric socket, jumping from a high place, drinking an unknown substance, teasing an animal, going into deep water, and walking off with a stranger are just a few of the ways children can be hurt. Parents above all else need to train their child to think and behave realistically in order to avoid danger.

The <u>Essential Parenting</u>™ trained parents know that their child's survival and prosperity depend upon his ability to understand the world the way it is, not the way he would like it to be. The fact is most parents will die before their children, and thus have a moral responsibility to train their children to overcome life's obstacles. They cannot pretend that the parents will always be around to hand carry the child over each and every obstacle that arises. The most devastating experience in life for a parent is living through the death of a child, so parents must work diligently to try and keep the child safe.

The modern-confused parent believes that if his child is given everything she wants then she will be happy, and eventually successful. In reality, the opposite is true. The child becomes handicapped as the parents attempt to meet the child's ever increasing demands without training the child how to resolve her own dilemmas in reaching her goals. In fact, the modern-confused parent through this appeasement process creates an emotionally confused and neurotic individual who believes she is entitled to have her wants met by others. To further compound the problem, the modern-confused parents attempt to shield their child from the harsh reality of life's unfairness.

They talk about how much better life is for the rich and powerful and if they were rich everything would be different. They fail to point out that being rich and powerful brings a different set of problems, that work is required for success, and that there really are evil people out there and evil forces to be avoided. The fact is that facing reality head-on teaches invaluable truths needed to reach greater heights in life's journey. To avoid, deny, pretend or create an illusionary world where these realities are eliminated is not an act of kindness by a parent, but an act of selfishness. This selfishness has lead to the development of a "new age" neurotic: an angry, self-centered, demanding, emotionally immature child unable to fend for himself in a world that does not revolve around

132

him, but exists for us to learn about and try to live with other in harmony.

EP trained parents have to commit Quantity Time and energy into training offspring in the dangers, nuances, and paradoxes of the real world. It is easier for a parent to provide video games and other material goods for the child rather than conscientiously train the child in developing skills and strategies to manage the world in which the child will be living. Evil psychopathic people exist who will molest and injure a child for their own satisfaction with no regard for the damage done to the child. A child needs to be warned about these evils in society and the parents need to vigilantly protect the child from these evils until he is able to protect himself.

For modern-confused parents to establish a high level of affluence for their children without giving the child the tools to maintain this level when the parents are no longer willing or able to do it is a cruel, selfish act, not a loving one. The modern-confused parent avoids teaching the child reality and the means of handling it instead creating a false sense of security by perpetuating the fantasy that the world will bow to the wishes of the "precious child". Without reality training a child is precariously positioned for a high impact crash into reality. Facing reality gives children the means to face life head on with the tools they will need to become successful adults.

# REALITY TRAINING

| ESSENTIAL PARENTING™ | MODERN-CONFUSED PARENTING |
|---|---|
| Teaches distinction between roles and power of parent and child | Creates the illusion of equality of roles and power of parent and child |
| Teaches that TV shows and videos are fantasy by viewing with child | Allows belief in fantasy |
| Defines problems and attempts to solve them | Avoids, denies or pretends problems do not exist |
| Teaches life is difficult for everyone regardless of their station in life | Thinks other's lives are better than theirs |
| Teaches to appreciate the reality of life | Teaches to appreciate the power of money and what it can buy |
| Teaches life is not fair | Allows child to fantasize that life should be fair |
| Knows there is good and evil, attempts to protect child from evil | Wants to believe child can make adult choices and consent to adult sexual behavior |
| Teaches that reality motivates to reach higher levels of self-fulfillment | Attempts to create an illusion that fantasy can bring happiness |
| Teaches that a child has to earn what he gets to gain personal satisfaction | Encourages child to think that he should be given everything he wants to insure happiness |

America is one of the most materialistically prosperous societies in the history of man. Disney World, television, movies, marketing, an average of $50 a week allowance for young children, and Christmases that begin in August are only a few of the indicators of a country based on fantasy thinking rather than an appreciation of reality. When disasters occur like hurricanes, wild fires, earthquakes, depression, illness, a horrible accident, or the death of a loved one, fantasy fades and reality takes center stage. No matter how much cement, plastic, or neon lights are used, reality is on the edge ready to take over. To conspire with Hollywood to perpetuate the illusionary world without preparing the child to deal with the inevitable harsh twists and turns of life is irresponsible on the part of the parent.

134

The confused parent on one hand allows a child to make choices the child is not prepared to make in the social and sexual area while on the other hand attempts to soften reality through fostering one fantasy after another. In either case, the confused parent's attempt to ignore reality means losing the valuable opportunities to train their child and to increase the child's awareness of how the world functions. Thus, the child is deprived of an edge in overcoming the real obstacles of life. When modern-confused parents align themselves with the marketers of fantasy, the child's behavior may be temporarily diverted, but in the long run it is not in the parent's or the child's best interest. The child needs to be prepared to leave the nest. Reality Training is indispensable for a child's successful departure. Also essential is the guiding inner voice called "a conscience" which must be developed to protect the child.

## CONSCIENCE TRAINING

*"Don't you see that that blessed conscience of yours is nothing but other people inside of you."*   Luigi Pirandello

Parents are primarily responsible for developing the conscience of their child. This is a sacred responsibility because it protects the child from destructive acts towards himself and others. It is true that a parent can create an overwhelmingly restrictive conscience that can paralyze an individual from "living life". Instead the individual takes on the guilt of the world and over analyzes his every action, in other words, becomes a neurotic. On the other hand, to eliminate the possibility of producing neurotics, our experts have gone to the other extreme and have practically removed all guilt from child rearing. Unfortunately, this has laid fertile ground for an epidemic of sociopaths. The answer is a balance between too much and too little. A reasonable and calibrated dose of guilt is necessary in developing and maintaining a healthy and spontaneous, yet socially sensitive individual.

Developing a conscience in your child is putting into place an historically tested human guidance system that will direct and protect your child from becoming insensitive and self-centered or worse, a sociopathic/evil individual. The Golden Rule: "Doing Unto Others As You Want Them To Do Unto You", a maxim found in some form in all religions, by definition teaches one to respect and cherish the life of oneself and others. The Ten Commandments clearly tell us what we should not do. When the parents practice the Golden Rule and the Ten Commandments, the child benefits. When the child believes the enforcement of these rules is for his benefit, and not for the status of the parent, a strong foundation for conscience development has been established.

If the parents do not commit themselves to consistently enforce these laws of moral behavior, the child will not understand that the sweet taste of misbehavior he receives in the short run will turn bitter in the long run. In other words, the child will not learn that lying, stealing, and disrespecting others will eventually have serious negative consequences on him. It is the parent's responsibility, by instructing the child through moral lessons, to keep the child on the time-tested path of our ancestral wisdom. These lessons will be resented and the opposite behavior will be deviously practiced if the child feels the parent only wants to impress the community by what a great parent she is. The upbringing of the preacher's son, for example, is often fraught with pitfalls because the child may view his preacher father's high expectations as unreasonable and unrealistic non-caring, self-serving parental behavior.

The values and virtues taught by the Golden Rule and Ten Commandments need to be seen as a gift. They function as the moral compass that will guide an individual in living a healthy, honorable and spiritual life. By praying together as a family every day and giving thanks to God for things like a beautiful sunset, flowers, good food, good health, clean water, a good night's sleep, family, and friends, children learn to appreciate what is really important in life. Appreciation of life is the antidote for depression and the key to good mental health.

Besides teaching appreciation parents have an obligation to protect their children from harmful influences. These influences may vary from inappropriate exposure to the media, to unruly children, to unstable or even evil individuals. A child needs parental guidance and set limits in this immoral, unstructured, chaotic, and confusing world. The child left to her own devices through permissiveness is without limits and will experiment and experience too much of reality before she has developed the wherewithal to protect herself from the destructive forces in life.

The modern-confused parent has erroneously accepted hook, line, and sinker the idea that if the parent provides "unconditional love/positive reinforcement" and material goods the child will be miraculously transformed into a "healthy adult". To impose one's religious beliefs, value system, expectations and standards on a child is to overburden the natural unfolding of this "perfect adult" inside the child. Transgressions by the child are overlooked because the child will learn on his own what is right or wrong and good or bad. The child is not required to contribute to the family or society since the child is " special". The parents and society are supposed to cater to the child. This cultural relativistic nonsense is a perfect prescription to raise a guiltless, self-centered, sociopathic adult. Home invasions, indiscriminate school shootings, rapes, car-jackings, drive-by shootings, and muggings are products of the cultural relativity non-conscience developing belief system. The instilling of a healthy conscience in our youth is the way to reverse the tide of senseless violence and evil.

137

# CONSCIENCE DEVELOPMENT

| ESSENTIAL PARENTING™ | MODERN-CONFUSED PARENTING |
|---|---|
| Role models Ten Commandments and Golden Rule | Overlooks child's transgressions |
| Teaches and insists on values such as truth, honor, justice, and integrity | Gives unconditional love regardless of behavior |
| Prays together as family | Relies on materialism and positive reinforcement |
| Teaches moral lessons based on child's behavior | Is unaware of or excuses child's transgressions |
| Teaches appreciation for what they have | Takes for granted and asks for more |
| Has high expectations and standards | Uses cultural relativism, unfair to child to expect anything |
| Shields from bad influences | Frees child to experiment and leaves to own devices |
| Teaches the need to contribute to society | Role models taking what you can get, use the system |

The development of a conscience is a protective defense against these destructive urges in ourselves and against immoral people who prey on the weak and innocent. The conscience begins to develop as soon as the parent states to the child this or that is good or bad. "It is good for you to help Mommy by getting your sister's diaper." "It is bad to bite your brother." A significant incident has to be followed by a "Just Right Moral Consequence". The child who helped with the diaper may be given the positive consequence of staying up a little later to hear a story after being told what a good girl she was in helping her mother. The child who bit his brother needs to be questioned to find out:
1. Did he actually bite his brother?
2. What he was thinking when he bit his brother?

If the child admits to doing the deed, no further investigation needs to be done. However, if there is a discrepancy between his story and the version given by others, including the parents' perception, an investigation ought to be started. After the investigation the parents should reach a "Just" decision. If he lied, there needs to be a strong negative consequence for continuing the lie, as well as a strong positive consequence for telling the truth. After the truth surfaces, the next step is to determine what the child was thinking when he did the deed. If the child is close in age to infancy and had no intention of hurting the brother you have one type of consequence, and if he meant to hurt his brother you have a more severe "Just Right Moral Consequence." (*See Chapter 4 JRMC section for detailed instruction.*)

These concrete and simple moral lessons start a progression of value and virtue lessons that lead to the abstract concept of justice, honor, responsibility, truth, and the acceptance of the Golden Rule and the Ten Commandments. The establishment of these values and everyday high standards of behavior is the framework of the conscience. The pain of guilt ties the framework together to make a viable force to repel self-destructive urges and evilness in society. When the child commits a wrong act, a gut reaction and/or an inside voice should direct the child to seek out a parent to confess his misdeed and sincerely ask for forgiveness. The parent directs the child on the path of correcting his misdeed.

The gut feeling and inner condemning voice are created by the parent's disapproval and expression of disappointment in the child's behavior as well as the pain the parent metes out to the child to create the connection between the misbehavior and pain. In essence, the parent communicates to the child that the child's misbehavior profoundly hurts the people he loves and is serious because God's laws or the laws of universal goodness have been broken as well. Rational and proportional guilt is based on how one's actions can negatively impact the people we love. Thus, guilt is the implicit recognition of the connection among all people.

# CREATING RATIONAL AND CALIBRATED GUILT FOR THE MISDEED

*"Guilt is the gift that keeps on giving."* *Erma Bombeck*

- Internalize morals, values, high expectations, and standards
- Disapproval and disappointment by parents
- Use of consequence to create misdeed-pain association
- Instruction of the affect of misdeeds on significant others
- Child exhibits remorseful apology, states "I will not do it again," and makes restitution

The "pain" the parent metes out to the child creates a misbehavior-pain association. After administering the necessary dose of "pain" the parents instruct the child how the particular behavior has negatively impacted others he respects and loves. Then they demonstrate to the child through instruction that his misdeed cannot be minimized and dismissed. The parent explains the adverse effect on others proving the gravity of the act. The child acknowledges the misdeed by giving a specific and detailed account of the act and its impact on others and finally remorsefully apologizes to all who were affected by the misdeed and states "I will never do it again."

Any recurring thought of these or similar types of misdeed would automatically result in a negative gut feeling and an inner voice telling him the deed is wrong and he should not do it again. The negative gut feeling is commonly called "guilt" while the inner voice saying "do not do it" is called our "conscience".

Using guilt proportional to the misdeed increases the intensity of the voice of our conscience and the pain in our gut that deters us from hurting others or ourselves. A child can know cognitively what is right and wrong without doing the right thing. Guilt is the motivator of the conscience. The greater the level of reasonable and calibrated guilt, the greater the likelihood the child will follow his conscience and do what is right. An individual can never be too moral for a family, community or nation. An individual who is moral in a moral family will reap dividends, but will risk exploitation in an immoral family, community, or nation. In the long run a moral person in an immoral community will suffer pain, but will have greater opportunity to avoid the pitfalls of a deviant lifestyle.

We need to establish and maintain our highest morals and standards, but calibrate our dose of guilt. It is true that too much guilt can immobilize and incapacitate an individual and cause depression. To be guilty for things beyond your control is an untenable position. Parents can selfishly create overwhelming guilt to control their child for their own benefit. "You cannot continue in school because the family needs you to earn money." This abuse of guilt has led many psychological experts to conclude that all guilt is negative.

In fact, the lack of guilt produces a self-centered, sociopathic society. When carefully calibrated guilt is used for developing a conscience and is a good mental health practice. The individual with a conscience has a moral compass by which to navigate the temptations and forces of life. An individual with a developed conscience can be trusted to do what is right when no one is watching. The moral conscience is a universally agreed upon set of standards of behavior which are programmed by the parent into the child, which allows everyone to live in greater harmony. Closely aligned although separate from conscience development is the important ability to sense the feelings of others.

# EMPATHY TRAINING

*"There, but for the grace of God, go I."*  *Anonymous*

*"I complained that I had no shoes until I met a man who had no feet."*  *Persian Proverb*

Empathy is the ability to sense how another person feels in a given situation. American Indians speak about "walking in another's moccasins" as empathy. Increased sensitivity to the feelings of others assists an individual in better understanding the human forces around us.

Children face obstacles in their young lives such as not doing something as well as a sibling or friend, becoming ill, a perceived or real imperfection, or delayed development. It appears teasing is a natural phenomenon which all humans experience. These experiences should be explored in order to bring out the feelings of the initial discomfort, feelings of inferiority, and pain associated with not measuring up to the ideal of oneself and others. The struggle of overcoming the adversity, admittedly discouraging at times should be embraced by the parents for the potential it has to offer to teach the child the importance of perseverance in conquering problems.

Occasionally parents use their power to lessen their child's inner pain by directly interfering in the child's peer group. This may offer temporary relief, but does nothing to assist the child in developing self-reliance. Adversity needs to be tackled head on, not be avoided by joining an "in group" that puts down others in attempting to hide their own self doubts. Strength of character comes from overcoming limitations, which gives the confidence needed to handle the next problem. The ridicule and harassment that a child encounters during the course of overcoming adversity can be a future gift in understanding human behavior. If the parent helps the child understand the people making fun of him are insecure and ignorant, he will be inoculated against becoming "one of them".

Whenever the parent sees another person being "put down" by someone, the parent needs to point this out to the child and remind him of his feelings when someone else ridiculed him. This personal pain from an earlier experience coupled with this current harassment of someone else will create empathy in the child. As the child's empathy grows so will the urge to protect and admire people fighting to overcome their limitations in life. This will inspire the individual in his struggle to become a genuine self-reliant person. A child needs to go through his own trials and tribulations before he can become sensitive to the experiences of others.

## EMPATHY TRAINING

| ESSENTIAL PARENTING™ | MODERN-CONFUSED PARENTING |
|---|---|
| Helps child accept own imperfections | Sees own child as perfect |
| Embraces adversity in order to teach character | Runs interference for child to avoid adversity |
| Points out the insensitivity of others towards people in general | Is too involved with other things or minimizes the harassment of one to another |
| Connects child's pain with the pain of others | Focuses on minimizing child's pain without noting pain of others |
| Encourages the child's urge to protect and admire people who accept and overcome their limitations | Encourages child to fit in by joining the group at the expense of others |
| Supports child's fight to be unique | Encourages child to blend in |

The confused parent perceives pain as having no positive value and attempts to eliminate it or at least to minimize it. To dedicate oneself to the elimination of pain is to attempt to deny reality by creating a fantasy. Reality possesses many types of pain. Pain is an indicator that there is something that needs to be adjusted, something to be learned.  Confused parents buy the child what they want or allow them to have friends or go with groups with whom the child should not be associated, so as not to face the psychological pain of not belonging.  Since we as humans are all unique we need to teach our children how to deal with pain, not attempt to shield them, which allows growth potential in overcoming and conquering greater and greater obstacles in life.  Pain is inevitable in life and parents ought to teach their children how to handle it.

## PAIN TRAINING

*"When pain ends, gain ends too."*  Robert Browning

A child needs to learn to deal with pain in order to be successful in life.  There is the psychological and emotional pain of failure or not getting what you want.  There is also the physical pain of illness or accident.  Pain is inevitable in life and is an early warning system that quickly informs us of an attack on our body, mind, or spirit.  Numbing pain with drugs, accidental neurological damage, or medically prescribed nerve blocks leaves the individual less aware of the surrounding environment and thus vulnerable to possible harm.  A parent's overprotection of a child to eliminate any pain will produce a fearful, neurotic child who will miss many natural experiences, which would challenge and strengthen her being.  When parents teach their child to accept the inevitability of pain and teach skills to control pain, the child will be more able to explore the world without the inhibiting fear of feeling pain.

In order to train a child in handling pain the parent has to understand the inevitability of pain and the benefits to the individual of facing and conquering pain.  Often misguided and confused parent's protective urge unconsciously eliminates little challenges that maintain the uncertainty and fearfulness of an overprotected child. A healthy and confident child is encouraged by his parents to overcome his fears by setting goals and working to satisfying them. The more difficult the attainment of the goal the greater the personal satisfaction. In other words, the greater the pain endured in reaching the objective the more profound is the development of the individual's inner strength.

The Essential Parenting™ trained parent through the POISE process is consistently monitoring and evaluating the child's ability to manage the intensity and duration of the obstacle and its resulting pain. The parent is the "gate keeper" allowing the child to experience gradually increasing levels of difficulty. Never place a child in a situation that might devastate him. As the child develops the confidence that he can tolerate and conquer pain, the greater becomes his scope of facing the world. A confident, courageous and competent child has the ingredients that would make any parent proud and creates a wonderful legacy to be left by the parent.

Theodore Roosevelt's overcoming of frailty in his early years through self-discipline has been an inspiration to many individuals worldwide. Retaining the knowledge that intellectual, emotional, and physical strength is only gained through the pain of hard effort will allow parents to embrace pain as a teaching tool to enhance the strength of their offspring. Problems are inevitable in life and by definition cause a certain amount of pain. A pain-free society of Prozac, Zoloft, Ritalin, alcohol, methadone, Ecstasy, and so on creates dependent and weak individuals who retreat from pain and fail to gain the inner confidence of resolving life's problems. This painless approach to living produces a weak individual, family and society

# PAIN TRAINING

| ESSENTIAL PARENTING™ | MODERN-CONFUSED PARENTING |
|---|---|
| Accepts that pain is inevitable and has to be taught how to manage it | Thinks pain is to be avoided at all costs |
| Identifies and faces problems the child is having | Shields child from problems, "sweeps under the rug" |
| Encourages child to take challenges that may result in pain | Shelters child to prevent possibility of pain |
| Calmly accepts the child's reasonable discomfort or pain from accident or social situations | Overreacts to child's pain communicating that child cannot handle pain |
| Encourages child to set goals and maintain effort | Gives the child what he wants without effort |
| Views the pain of problem solving as positive character development | Views pain as negative and attempts to remove it |
| Helps child calmly describe pain size, color, intensity- imagery of pain, control pain by confronting it visualizing the decrease of pain | Uses all means to remove the pain- local anesthesia, general pain killers or psychotropic drugs |
| Shows the child the pain can be modulated by focusing on other things- mind over matter | Thinks pain should not have to be endured by their child |

In order for an individual to get what she desires she will have to endure the pain of obtaining the goal. Will power is the ability of an individual to focus and persevere in her pursuit of a specific purpose or goal without allowing anything to distract her from accomplishing the purpose or goal.

# WILL POWER TRAINING

*"Life is something like a trumpet. If you don't put anything into it you don't get anything out."  W. C. Handy*

*Winners never quit and quitters never win.  American Saying*

If you want something and are willing to pay the price of mental and physical energy, you can obtain it. Throughout our adult lives we see certain people do extraordinary things in education, business, war, sports, by focusing all their energy until they have reached their goal. People have relearned how to move after paralysis, become renowned intellectuals after being born into an illiterate family, reached great athletic heights even with physical handicaps. These individuals have applied perseverance and dedication to overcome major obstacles.

Will Power most often has its foundation in the child rearing process. Parents create the environment, which will teach a child that either he can do anything he sets his sights on, or that he requires others to provide him with what he wants. Essential Parenting™ trained parents start with a simple task for their child which is accurately completed and progress onto harder and harder tasks that challenge the child's interest and ability. The parent monitors the successful completion or gives encouragement and suggestions but never completes the task for the child. The EP trained parents build on the interest of the child for the sake of the child, not living their lives through their child as you often see with overbearing parents. The EP trained parents are constantly keeping in mind their child's self interest, not their own.

The child is required to earn privileges or rewards since giving privileges without effort misses the opportunity to learn the habit of success. The child learns through this habit of success to tackle other problems and resolve them. In other words, the parent gives the child the experience and knowledge that through mental and physical perseverance life can be dealt with head-on. Simultaneously Essential Parenting™ is instilling morals, values, goals and expectations as soon as circumstances allow. The inculcating of morals and values in a child guides the child from material goals to more spiritual goals. This guidance directs the individual to a higher level, more meaningful pursuit that continues the challenge of enlarging the scope of a person's control over her destiny.

147

# WILL POWER TRAINING

| ESSENTIAL PARENTING™ | MODERN-CONFUSED PARENTING |
|---|---|
| Expects child to accomplish simple tasks followed by more difficult ones | Expects and demands little of child |
| Monitors child and administers consequences if child does not meet expectations and standards | Bails child out, it is easier to do it myself |
| Makes child earn material privileges by demonstrating good work habits | Provides material things and privileges the parent never had |
| Encourages child to set own goals and work toward them | Gives into the ever increasing demands of the child or lives through their child |
| Decreases monitoring and accepts child as an adult | Attempts to increase monitoring as child approaches adolescence |

Modern-confused parents ironically attempt to discipline their child at the least opportune time when the child approaches adolescence. By this stage of development many bad habits need to be reversed which becomes a monumental endeavor. If parents discipline their child from infancy the child is trained to have strong, healthy behavioral patterns in accepting and utilizing love, to be obedient, respectful, honest, be grounded in reality, have a conscience, be empathetic and understand pain in his life. These externally transmitted behavioral patterns are the foundation necessary for the child to move into adulthood by developing will power. Once an individual has internalized will power, the young adult is able to launch herself into the world outside the family unit.

# DEVELOPING CREATIVITY

*Every animal leaves traces of what it was; man alone leaves traces of what he created. Jacob Bronowski*

Parents should provide a physical and emotional environment where a child's creativity can flourish. Every child being unique will express her creativity in a different form. One child may use Lego Blocks to demonstrate perceptual creativity, another may

148

beat on various objects to hear the creative sound they make, another child may demonstrate fine motor coordination drawing creative pictures, another gracefulness in motion demonstrating their creativity in dance or sports.

The Essential Parenting™ parents focus on the child through observation (see POISE process) to determine her natural inclination and then prepare the home environment to increase the opportunities for the child to have experiences that will stimulate her creative urges. The more Quantity Time parents spend and are more aware of what enhances creativity in their child the more effective their anticipating the creative needs of their child. Once the parents understand what are creative endeavors for their child, the parents should eliminate any comments that may be interpreted by the child as not meeting expectations of the parents. At the same time they should allow and subtly encourage the child's necessary long intervals of concentration to perfect his creative skills

## DEVELOPING CREATIVITY

| ESSENTIAL PARENTING™ | MODERN-CONFUSED PARENTING |
|---|---|
| Gives validity to child's sincere endeavors. Spends Quantity Time. | Unaware of child's creative urges or pushes the child in particular direction which meets parent's needs. |
| Provides blank paper, crayons, pencils, and markers for child's use. | Provides coloring book and crayons. |
| Asks the child to tell you about their drawings. | Parent says what the picture looks like, may not be anything like what the child drew. |
| Lets child help in making cookies by selecting toppings, shapes. | Purchases cookies in store. |
| Encourages child to write picture stories with parents writing words. | Buys the latest toy, movie or video game for child. |
| Helps child to select projects of interest where they can use their creative energies: to design and plant a flower garden, make crafts, build a walkway. | Puts child in extra curricular activity, watches television or plays with electronic entertainment. |

These creative guidelines will only be useful with parents who have sufficient time, Quantity Time, with their child. The modern-confused parents use of quality time will not provide enough opportunity to be exposed to the child over time and in many settings. Thus, responsible, emotionally mature people strive to perfect their knowledge and awareness to better meet the needs of their children. This striving to be a better adult is necessary for the next less concrete phase of love between child and parent which is essential and underlying all Purposeful Discipline.

Through the PURPOSEFUL DISCIPLINING SYSTEMATIC TRAINING components of: loving training, obedience training, independence training, potty training, respectfulness training, honesty training, conscience training, empathy training, pain training, will power training, developing creativity, and reality training parents have learned how to be in charge of their family's destiny.

Essential Parenting™ training is a lifetime process that places the responsibility of child rearing squarely in the hands of parents. As trained parents gain experience with their children, their absolute confidence and awareness should expand. This on-going perfecting of one's parenting is an essential element of Essential Parenting™ training. Parenting has to be constantly evaluated to keep the trained parent on the right path in this maze of choices in developing healthy children.

# Chapter 6

## Perfecting Your Parenting:
### CRITERIA FOR EVALUATING YOUR TRAINING PROGRAM

*"A child is the father of the man."* William Wordsworth

*"It is a wise father that knows his own child."*
William Shakespeare

The development of the child allows the parents to relive or review their own childhood, giving parents the opportunity to become healthier and better functioning adults. "My children raised me well" is one of the dividends of being a conscientious parent. The other part is equally important: raising children you are proud to call your own. A drill sergeant knows how he wants a new recruit to act at the end of basic training, like a soldier. A parent should know how the child should act at the end of "child-rearing", a decent human being similar to themselves.

Not experts, nor books, nor television shows, neither magazines, nor scientific studies are essential for you to know how well you are doing as a parent. Evaluating and perfecting your parenting is done through your studied observations. The observation of your

151

child's specific behaviors and developmental progress allows the parent concrete feedback to understand which strategy is beneficial and which is not. This PARENTAL OBSERVATIONAL–INDICATION-STRATEGIZATION-EVALUATION provides quality assurance to the parents on the development of their child. POISE is an on-going process that fine-tunes the parents' interaction with their child.

The key to evaluating and perfecting your parenting is to:
> **deploy** the essential building blocks of a functioning family
> **track** whether the child meets minimum standards of behavior
> **determine** if the child possesses socially approved character traits
> **self-review** your parenting effort
> **observe** (using POISE) the ongoing behavior of the child in order to develop and modify strategies and tactics to keep the child on course.

The child reaching certain social standards and expectations, the existence or non-existence of essential building blocks and POISE provide the necessary data for evaluating and perfecting parenting skills.

## CHILD DEVELOPMENT MILESTONES:
## TIME TABLE OF EXPECTATIONS FOR CHILDREN

Our ancestors have developed some standards and expectations over time. These milestones include:

| | |
|---|---|
| Talking | one to two years |
| Walking | nine to eighteen months |
| Obeying simple commands | six months to one year |
| Feeding self | nine months to one year |
| Sitting in a chair | seven months to one year |
| Dressing self | two to two and 1/2 years |
| Potty training | eighteen months to two 1/2 years |

## ESSENTIAL BUILDING BLOCKS OF A WELL FUNCTIONING FAMILY:

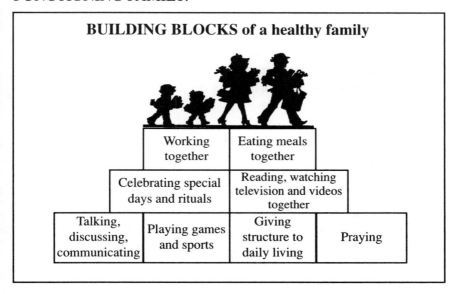

**BUILDING BLOCKS of a healthy family**

| | | | |
|---|---|---|---|
| | Working together | Eating meals together | |
| | Celebrating special days and rituals | Reading, watching television and videos together | |
| Talking, discussing, communicating | Playing games and sports | Giving structure to daily living | Praying |

As the child evolves reaching the milestones in life, so does a family evolve. The traditional family starts with husband and wife learning to adjust to each other. When a baby arrives the parents again readjust to incorporate the new family member. This means new routines and structures are developed and old ones altered. This happens every time a new child arrives. Parents need to make a significant time commitment to create a healthy family culture. A large chunk of time, Quantity Time, has to be devoted to eating together, playing, working, praying, and communicating with each other.

Initially eating may be nursing or bottle-feeding for the infant and then expanding to finger food at the table and eventually eating with utensils. The progression of the stages of eating is a wonderful opportunity to laugh and smile- appreciating time together. Pleasurable time spent as a family around the dinner table enjoying delicious, nutritious food and each other's company

153

helps create strong bonds between the family members. Eating together is a wonderful time to educate your children. Parents communicate the family's historical beginnings and anecdotes. The child can be given the opportunity to tell what she learned that day while the parents share their own experiences of their day. General knowledge as well as moral and value training are only a few of the educational opportunities offered around the dinner table.

Throughout history feasting together with family and friends has been an essential, almost sacred element of celebrations and holidays. The damage done to the American family by no longer eating together has been ignored for convenience in our hectic life style. Not only are elaborate meals mostly a memory, but many family members eat by themselves in and out of the home. Today the opportunity for role modeling and training experiences is considerably decreased. A healthy family intuitively or consciously maximizes role modeling and training opportunities by dining together as often as possible.

Working together as a family is another means of parents having an opportunity to learn about and train their children. Mothers or fathers can spend time in the kitchen teaching their child simple to more complex skills. The parent can start the child cutting up vegetables at the age of three and continue increasing the participation to making simple dishes by grating cheese and pouring milk and the cheese on cooked macaroni. Before they become teenagers children can cook complete dinners if they have been given the opportunity to learn. There are projects inside and outside the house such as cleaning, sewing, painting, baking, making crafts, gardening, building, raking, and pruning that family members can do together. As the children physically mature the projects can become more sophisticated like tiling floors, working on motors and adding room additions which allow the child to see the results which come from individuals working together as well as learning important life skills.

Instead of everyone in the family going their own direction with one parent chauffeuring children from one venue to another, the family needs to do activities together to create positive memories of these family experiences. These happy memories can be as mundane as watching a favorite television show together, making pizza from scratch, playing a board game, or visiting relatives and friends, or as big as a camping experience, or a family vacation. As these snapshots of having fun together increase so does the allegiance and warmth of the family members toward each other.

Family memories can cluster around special family interests such as gardening, dancing, sport activities, travel, a business venture or whatever interests the particular individuals. The parents normally establish the interest and everyone is required to participate. The participation may be enthusiastic or reluctant although all share the experience repeatedly over time. After a number of these experiences the child accepts the inevitable and joins in with the family. The limiting of choices as happens in economic depression forces family members tightly together for survival reasons, creating a greater interdependence. Often the child may even come back to enjoy the activity in the same way a child may learn to like a food after trying it several times.

Difficult situations where everyone "pitches in" in response to the unpredicted event create a feeling of closeness in the family. Everyone pushing when the car gets stuck, making a meal without electricity when the lights go out, unclogging an overflowing sink, fixing a leak on the roof, cooking and cleaning when Mom is sick, taking care of the neighbor's home and pets when an emergency arises are important lessons in life which are never forgotten. The accumulation of these memorable picture memories is the glue that keeps the family together.

Well functioning families learn the necessity of establishing structure, routine, rituals and traditions for the well being of family members. Structure and routine keep everyone on a schedule and rhythm that maximizes long range productivity, physical, mental and spiritual health. A child develops a natural sleeping and eating schedule. A mother quickly learns that anything that interrupts the child's routine leaves the child cranky and irritable. This is why parents need to initially establish a routine and schedule that they can live with over time or pay a heavy price in attempting to change it at a later time.

It is for this reason that an infant or child should not sleep in the parent's bed but instead be trained to sleep in his own bed from infancy. A child should be required to go to sleep at a reasonable hour so the parents will have time to communicate with each other for awhile and still have ample hours of sleep. Inconsistent sleep patterns have a negative physical and mental implication for any individual regardless of age, but especially for a young child. The more consistent eating time is during the day, the better the body can regulate the blood sugar level. Consistence in eating and sleeping helps the individual maintain mental and physical health.

Parents often develop a bedtime ritual for children of taking a bath, reading a story, saying prayers that clearly and methodically ready the child for a night's rest. A close knit family passes down customs from one generation to another. It may be as specific as how to prepare certain foods to a series of directives on how to celebrate a holiday. There are special dishes for certain holidays and many ceremonial acts that are handed down from parents to children. These bedtime and mealtime rituals coupled with holiday traditions bring everyone together.

The way a birthday is celebrated makes family interaction joyful. The manner of getting the gift, when to give the presents, the type of foods used to celebrate, what kind of cake and candles are unique in many families. Yearly family activities are often great memories for a family. Opening up the summer cottage, going to a sporting event, harvesting crops from the garden, decorating the home, holiday shopping, a family vacation, baking cookies, shopping for an updated computer or new car are shared activities.

The daily responsibilities are usually handled individually, not by the entire family. A parent taking the time to train children in family chores is an excellent sign of a vibrant family. Bringing a child into the role of helping other members of the family gives him more of a stake in the family and teaches him the skills and habits necessary for his future success. The contribution initially will be limited to getting a diaper for the new baby but will increase in complexity to driving the lawnmower or cooking dinner, challenging the child's interests and skill level. The monitoring of the child decreases as the instilled responsible habits are exhibited. If there is fairness in the distribution of the chores amongst children and parents then chores have a bonding effect on the family. When a child is not being exploited and sees the results of the contribution her chores make to the family, then chores are viewed as an inevitable part of life. The child learns to view her chores as her contribution to the family.

The interdependence of family members is no better illustrated than when a family member becomes ill. It can be a parent caring for a child or spouse or a child nurturing a sibling or responding to the illness of a parent. The reaction of a parent to the sick child can have a profound impact on the child's disease. An over-reaction by the parent can cause the child to feel overwhelmed. The child is able to read the body language of the parent which is often more important than the parental words. The child sensing the parent's high level of anxiety or even panic can adversely affect the child's immune response to the disease.

On the other end of the disease process is the child who's recovery goes unrecognized by the parent who has been emotionally devastated by dealing with their child's illness. This situation leads to the child being pampered by the parent who cannot deal with the illness and limits the opportunity for growth. When a healthy child reaches out to another family member, sibling or parent, who is ill and eventually recovers the child learns the power of "being there" for one another. Giving energy, good thoughts and prayers to help a loved one is a powerful purpose that enriches all involved.

Gratitude, reverence and awe expressed through our prayers gives family members the highest purpose of a healthy life, belief in God. The strength gained through prayer enables families to endure worldly setbacks and helps individual family members to set their sights on spiritual endeavors rather than solely material pursuits. Praying to God clarifies what is truly important in one's life, providing the individual with inner spiritual and mental courage to make the right and necessary choices in life.

In the highly materialistic world which surrounds us our choices are concentrated on what we can do to earn the money which will allow us to purchase what we desire. Teaching our children spirituality and sharing our ancestral wisdom has been replaced by the gifts we use to buy the love of our child. When compared to the time spent in teaching our child how to live, material gift giving is uncaring. The gifts quickly lose their luster with the child leaving nothing in the child that will enable him or her to better deal with reality. In fact, the accumulation of material goods through gifts encourages a life style that becomes unattainable when the gifts stop through personal decision, financial misfortune, or death. Giving material gifts instead of imparting one's knowledge eventually becomes a cruel act.

# ESSENTIAL BUILDING BLOCKS OF FAMILY

| FUNCTIONING | NON FUNCTIONING |
|---|---|
| Quanity Time is spent among family members | Individual family members spend time away from each other and compensate through "quality time" |
| Family members eat together daily and exhibit a shared cluster of socially approved eating behavior | Family members eat separately and do as they wish |
| Family members work together sharing knowledge and effort accomplishing a common family purpose | Parents work isolated from children and do not make time to work together when at home |
| Family members pray together | Praying is not practiced |
| Recreational activities and visiting done together | Everyone does "their own thing" |
| Daily activities are structured and routines are established | Daily activities are accomplished whenever possible; often appears chaotic |
| Rituals and traditions are developed and practiced such as bedtime, eating rituals, holiday and travel traditions | Rituals and traditions have not evolved due to lack of commitment at home |
| Chores are shared by family members | Parents find it easier to do chores themselves |

## SPECIFIC CHILD BEHAVIOR:
*INDICATORS OF A HEALTHY CHILD BY NON PARENT EVALUATORS*

Your children are not only being evaluated by you as parents, but by everyone who crosses paths with them. These unpaid and uninvited appraisers of your child are found everywhere you bring your child, such as the supermarket, park playground, restaurant, church, shopping mall, school, office, and friend's and relative's homes. Most of the interaction between your child and these non-parent people are inconsequential and result in a fleeting glance as they pass each other. Whatever the reason there are times when people focus on your child and inevitably come up with a positive or negative impression. These impressions are often weak and imperceivable to others but a few are sufficiently intense to register and be communicated through body language especially in

159

facial expression: either an approving smile or a disapproving frown.

Only occasionally does the intensity reach a point where the outside individual actually verbalizes their evaluation of your child. The reactions of these non-parental individuals are a wonderful check and balance resource to our often parental bias, myopic view of our child. The feedback from others is there if we have the courage to honestly observe their reaction or even to solicit their opinions.

Our citizens are being insidiously trained by psychobabble experts in the media to lower or even remove standards to protect the few who cannot meet these standards because of physical defects or poor training. However the average citizen still possesses enough ancestral knowledge to know when a child he sees is a brat or well behaved.

The following is a list of specific behaviors. Those on the left when satisfied indicate a child is progressing in a healthy manner while those on the right send a red flag warning of serious problems ahead.

## MINIMUM STANDARDS AND EXPECTATIONS FOR A HEALTHY CHILD

| INDICATORS OF STABILITY | INDICATORS OF INSTABILITY |
|---|---|
| **Bedtime:** | |
| Sleeps in own bed | Sleeps in parent's bed |
| Remains in bed | Gets up several times |
| Has reasonable bedtime | Goes to bed when chooses |
| Follows family schedule | Demands another kiss, story, or drink |
| Undresses, dresses self | Waits to be dressed |
| Uses bathroom at night | Wets bed |
| Brushes teeth daily | Refuses to brush own teeth |
| Takes a bath daily | Refuses to bathe |

160

## Mealtime:

| | |
|---|---|
| Eats with entire family | Eats separately |
| Helps with food preparation | Does not consider helping |
| Sets table | Does not set table |
| Eats what is served | Picky eater |
| Talks with family | Yells and carries on |
| Eats properly with knife and fork | Eats with hands |
| Uses good manners | Refuses to use proper manners |

## Shopping

| | |
|---|---|
| Stays close by parents | Runs around store |
| Listens to parents | Throws tantrums |
| No demanding of parents to buy | Demands parent to buy this and that |
| Speaks in quiet voice | Yells and cries |

## Office

| | |
|---|---|
| Sits in chair | Wanders around office |
| Sits quietly | Demands attention |
| Listens without participating | Interrupts adults frequently |
| Follows direction of authority figure | Does not follow directions |

## Restaurant

| | |
|---|---|
| Sits quietly with family | Wanders around |
| Eats in mannerly way | Uses poor manners |
| Waits until everyone is finished | Leaves table when finished |
| Appreciates being able to eat out | Views eating out as an entitlement |

## School

| | |
|---|---|
| Listens to teachers | Is disruptive |
| Completes daily work | Makes excuses for not finishing work |
| Completes homework | Partially does homework or not at all |
| Follows directions | Not obedient |
| Is respectful to others | Troublemaker |

## At play

| | |
|---|---|
| Respects person and property | Hurts others and property |
| Plays fair | Cheats |
| Participates fully | Gives little or no effort |
| Accepts winning or losing with grace | Gloats or pouts |

## Chores

| | |
|---|---|
| Does without parent reminder | Needs constant reminders |
| Completes daily chores | Chores incomplete no effort |
| Takes pride in doing good work | Indifferent to result |

## SOCIALLY APPROVED CHARACTER TRAITS

The possessing of acceptable societal traits by the child is a sure sign that the parents are doing a credible job as a trainer of the child.

| ACCEPTABLE TRAITS | UNACCEPTABLE TRAITS |
| --- | --- |
| Obedient | Disobedient |
| Honest | Dishonest |
| Respectful | Disrespectful |
| Hard working | Lazy |
| Good sportsmanship | Sore loser |
| Compassionate | Selfish |
| Realistic | Unrealistic |
| Disciplined | Undisciplined |

These character traits are indicators of how well you are doing as a parent in spite of all the psychobabble to the contrary. This list can go on and on covering many more important traits we expect in our citizens. These good character traits have been passed down through generations giving us the necessary framework upon which to build a proper child. A parent's honest appraisal of whether or not the establishment of these traits has been manifested in their child is a quick and reliable means of determining whether the parent has done a viable job in their training.

## PARENTING SELF EVALUATION:

A parent not only has to look at their child's milestones, specific behavior, and feedback from others but must review and evaluate their own parental behavior. An honest review of these lists will assist a parent in determining their areas of strength and areas of concern.

## PARENTING SELF EVALUATION

| POSITIVE INDICATORS | NEGATIVE INDICATORS |
|---|---|
| Wants to spend time with child | Avoids spending time with child other things come first |
| Does what is promised | Does not keep promises to children |
| Interacts daily, nurturing, playing and training child | Leaves interaction with child to others |
| Requires and obtains behavior that may not be what the child wants | Pleases child regardless of long term negative consequences |
| Notes and stops child's attempts at manipulation using affection, crying, tantrums, shyness, fake sickness | Allows child to manipulate, thinks it is cute |
| Accepts the reality that the child will not always like them.  Relishes the opportunity to place limits | Strives to be liked by child |
| Says "no" to child as needed Understands a child is on a "temporary loan" until 18 years and has a limited time for training | Has difficulty saying "no" to child Either wants to rush maturity or expects child to be their "baby" forever |
| Possesses an identity and life interests besides the child | Lives their life through the child or totally away from the child |

The Parent Self-Evaluation is another element in evaluating the program established for one's child.  An honest appraisal of the implementation of your overall training program will give the parent a fair idea if you are on the right philosophical and behavioral track.  The ultimate gauge of one's parenting is the end product:  the child.

## THE USEFULNESS OF STRESS

Naturally stressful situations like illness, lack of sleep or missing a meal will bring out weak or unfinished areas of training.  Stress triggers the child to demonstrate his self-centered strategies both emotionally and behaviorally.  One child may become depressed or act mean while another may need more affection and the third may throw a tantrum in a stressful situation.  This natural stress coupled with purposefully putting a child in a situation where there is a high level of expectation such as on a sports team or performing in a play allows the parents an opportunity to see the positive result of their training and the need for future training.

A child who is able to perform well under stress is a healthier and better trained child than a child who breaks down under pressure. The parents can test their children by placing manageable, well thought out, achievable obstacles in front of the children and giving them support to overcome them. The child learns that through effort he can successfully conquer his problems. Thus through the parental observation and actual interaction with the child, the parents are constantly evaluating the child and revising their strategies in order to better carry out their Essential Parenting™.

**FINE TUNING THE TRAINING**

The child's behavior expands as he increasingly interacts outside the home. If the early training was correctly and solidly established, the child's development will proceed relatively uneventfully. As new milestones are reached and the world opens up to the child, new challenges will be met by building on the foundation begun in the early years. By using the Parental Observation-Indication-Strategization-Evaluation process the parent will fine-tune the training program to better meet the needs of the child.

If the child appears to be tentative, withdrawing into himself, a more relaxed approach can be used while a more restrictive strategy would be required when the child initiates testing parental limits. This fine turning is cyclical lasting for the duration of the child's training. These cycles are as unique as each child is unique. It appears that each child tends to possess an individual duration period for its cycle. It can be several months, weeks and for a problem child- daily. Once parents become aware of the

164

pattern they will be better prepared to anticipate their expenditure of energy to re-establish the parameters with the child.

Through Essential Parenting™ a parent can perfect his/her parenting by using the following criteria for evaluating:

> **deploy** the essential building blocks of a functioning family
> **track** whether the child meets minimum standards of behavior
> **determine** if the child possesses socially approved character traits
> **self-review** your parenting effort
> **observe** (using POISE) the ongoing behavior of the child in order to develop and modify strategies and tactics to keep the child on course.

Essential Parenting™ presents a philosophical rationale and systematic methodology for dealing with most major child rearing issues. Nevertheless, Essential Parenting™ cannot be and should not be a comprehensive cookbook for raising children. Child rearing has to be modified and tailored for each unique child. The principles and guidelines need to be used by Essential Parenting™ trained parents along with their intuition, instincts, sensitivity and ingenuity in providing the best learning and training environment for their children.

# Chapter 7

## Frequently Asked Questions

*"Most people spend more time and energy going around a problem than in trying to solve them."  Henry Ford*

Essential Parenting™ is rooted in the love of parents for their children.  At first the parental love is expressed by meeting the basic needs of the infant such as food, love, and shelter.  It subsequently grows into meeting more and more complex and abstract needs such as morals, values, and beliefs that will guide the child through life.  The world is on one hand beautiful and tranquil yet on the other hand brutal and unfair.  Parents by giving birth to a life are morally responsible to provide the environment for the optimal development of all areas of their child to maximize the child's ability to survive on his own and to become a decent, moral, contributing member of society.  Essential Parenting™ provides the blueprint needed for a parent to help the child develop into a fully functioning decent and contributing member of society.

Parents following the guidelines and principles of Essential

Parenting<sup>TM</sup> as outlined throughout the book will have already addressed many of the issues discussed in this chapter. Most of the solution's rationale can be traced back to specific text in the book. Whenever possible the reader is referred back to sections of the text to elaborate on the answer. The following is a list of the most Frequently Asked Questions and a possible solution to these concerns. This list of FAQ is not meant to be read before reading the previous chapters. Only in conjunction with the preceding text will the solutions have the intended impact.

QUESTION: What do I do when my child refuses to get dressed in the morning to be on time for school?

SOLUTION: You can first exhaust all normal positive interventions such as saying "I will reward you if you get dressed on time in the morning by taking you to the park after school." The opposite approach of saying, "You will lose the privilege of watching television every day that you are not dressed on time for school" is a direct consequence for such a behavior *(see Chapter 5: Obedience and Independence Training)*. Taking the child to school in his/her pajamas will have immediate dividends. The child will understand when you say, "get dressed" you mean it. Getting the child into the car or to the bus stop in her pajamas will usually end this "dressing game".

QUESTION: How do I stop my child from saying "no" to me?

SOLUTION: This is not a joking matter. A child two years old or younger appears to be cute and feisty, but remember your reaction, good or bad, will set a precedent for the future *(See Chapter 3: Establishing and Maintaining Control and Chapter 5: Obedience Training)*. Laughing or ignoring the child will send the message to the child that this is acceptable behavior. Remember that nipping this "in the bud" will save you a lot of aggravation in the long run.

A spank on the behind followed by a statement that "you do not say "no" to me" will repress or certainly make the child think twice before again speaking disrespectfully to her parent. If the child is older than two years of age the parent needs to "go to war" with the child (confront the child) and win by getting an apology from the child for his disrespect before ending the "war".

QUESTION: What do I do when my child lies directly to me after I observed him doing the misdeed?

SOLUTION: The lying needs to be directly addressed. The child needs to first admit the lie. Initially the problem causing the lie should be overlooked as long as the child tells the truth *(See Chapter 5: Honesty Training)*. When the child is young, from two to five years old, and the parent directly observes the child's behavior such as breaking something or hitting another child, the parent needs to focus on the child admitting the truth by ignoring the misdeed the child is attempting to deny by lying. "If you tell me the truth I will not punish you for breaking my dish but if you lie to me, I will give you a spanking or take _____ away from you for a week."
It should be made clear to the child that telling the truth will only have positive results and lying will only have negative results. Ask the child to admit the lie.
1. Role model telling the truth
2. Observe the child lying
3. Focus on the child admitting the truth while ignoring the behavior for which the child is lying.
4. Announce to the child there will be no punishment for whatever he did as long as he takes responsibility for it.
5. Request that the child admit to you she lied.

If the child is older than 6 earlier training has undoubtedly occurred. The situation where the child has not told the truth has previously occurred, perhaps many times.

1.  Make a thorough investigation if a credible individual accuses her of lying.
2.  If the evidence is convincing then mete out a consequence for the inappropriate behavior while encouraging the admission of the truth.
3.  If the truth is admitted continue the consequence for the behavior. Too many children think saying "I'm sorry" removes any possibility of punishment.
4.  Inform the child you are proud about his remorsefully admitting to the lie.
5.  Use your discretion in mitigating the severity of the consequence.
6.  If the child continues to lie use punishing consequence to make misdeed pain association.
7.  Child exhibits remorse, apologizes, states: "I will not do it again," and makes restitution.

QUESTION:  How do I get my child to do chores around the house?

SOLUTION:  A child needs to feel like a contributing member of the family to gain strength from the family.  Daily chores give the child a sense of worth and importance.  Chores are also valuable for developing responsible work habits in a child.

The effort expended by the parent in training the child is time well spent.  The child has to learn to follow simple then more complex commands.  A parent starts with an easy chore like picking up the toys and then progresses to more involved activities.  The parent initially carefully instructs and supervises the activity and then relies more on monitoring the end product and administering appropriate positive or negative consequences.

If the child refuses to do any chores it is an indicator of a more profound defiance issue.  It means the parents have to re-establish their power, "go to war", by refusing to do anything for the child. This battle should last for a brief interval depending on the determination of the parent. Whatever the child asks for, the parent's response would be " you do not want to do your part as a family member by helping out so I am not going to help you." That means no cooking for the child, washing clothes, driving him anywhere or doing anything else for him. The defiant child usually realizes quite quickly that defiance does not pay when the parent demonstrates his power.

QUESTION: How do you stop a child who bites another child?

SOLUTION: It is not unusual for a very small child to bite when a situation arises where he feels frustration. It is usually children who cannot communicate well who bite. The simplest and most efficient method of helping a child become empathetic to the pain of someone he has bitten is by experiencing pain by being slapped on the hand for biting. The old fashioned remedy for biting used to be having the parent bite the child back to show him how it feels. This still may be an effective antidote if it gives the child the message that biting is wrong and it hurts. The parent should ask the child how it felt to behurt and if he thought it is a good thing to hurt another person. He should answer it is bad to hurt or bite someone. If he does not respond this way the parent states it is bad to bite someone and the child repeats the sentence.

QUESTION: How do I react when my child repeats the same misbehavior shortly after being punished for it?

SOLUTION: The first thing the parent needs to do is increase the duration of the consequence or use a higher level consequence in order to stop the inappropriate behavior. A child who continues to do the inappropriate behavior shortly after being punished for it has not gotten the message that it should not be done. The child needs to be reminded very frequently why he is sitting in the chair while all his friends are out playing in the yard. When you walk by him sitting in a "time out" situation you need to remind him why he is sitting and have him repeat to you why he is sitting. It is important for the child to hear this often so he cannot ignore you and the reason he is under a disciplinary restriction.

QUESTION: What do I do when my child says, "I hate you"?

SOLUTION: When a child says, "I hate you" the parent responds in a matter of fact way, "of course you do not hate me" which eliminates any attempt at the child diverting the parent's attention from the consequence for the child's original misdeed. The parent continues with the behavioral consequence that preceded the outburst. If it was an effective consequence for the child it should be completed.

After dealing with the initial problem, the parent should address the "I hate you" issue by meting out an additional consequence for making that statement. Telling the child "how dare you talk to me that way", or "do not ever say that to me again" in a stern, firm tone of voice shows the child this is not something she should ever try again. Later the parent can explain to the child that he knows the child loves him but the parent will not accept disrespectful behavior. The child needs to clearly understand that saying, "I hate you" is not an acceptable thing to say to her parent.

QUESTION: What do I do when television watching is taken away as a consequence and the child replies she does not care if she ever watches television again?

SOLUTION: This is a ploy many children use. The child may act as if she does not care about not being able to watch her favorite television program (or listen to music or go out to play). This is only an act especially if the child exhibited an interest previously. When a program the child likes to see comes on the television the

171

parent should show a little of it and then turn it off. The parent should inform the child how much fun other children are having watching this show while the parent turns it off. The parent continues saying that since the child does not enjoy watching television it will not matter if she misses this show. Other siblings should continue to do what the disciplined child cannot such as watching the favorite program on television. The punished child should remain in the proximity but where she cannot see or hear the television.

QUESTION: What do I do when my child is not satisfied with her gift?

SOLUTION: If a child expresses dissatisfaction with a gift received for whatever reason, the gift should be taken away. No other gift should be substituted for the removed gift and other gifts she may have received as well could be removed. Until the child learns to express appreciation to her parents or other gift givers the child should not be given anything else. The child should be made to sincerely apologize for her crude behavior.

QUESTION: How do I get my child to stop continually interrupting me while I am speaking to another adult?

SOLUTION: First the parent has to see this as a problem. Many parents act as if their child's interruptions and their own patient response to the child's questions is a sign of positive parenting skill, which it is not. The fundamental problem is the child is not being taught appropriate limits. In addition, the child is hampering communication between the parent and the other adult. The parent needs to firmly tell the child to stop his interruptions because the parent is speaking to the other adult. If the child disobeys the directive, then the parent ought to realize his *Obedience Training* needs to be reviewed (*See Chapter 5*).

The child should be told how his interruptions are not considerate to the adults and be asked to leave the room. Later, after the visitor has left is a good time to have a stern talk with the child about this behavior, letting him know the consequences of a repeat of this behavior. As with any change in behavior the parents want to effect, they need to know what change they want and be firm and consistent until the behavior is changed.

QUESTION: How do I get my child to eat what is served to everyone else?

SOLUTION: The family expectation should be made clear that everyone is required to eat at least a small portion of what is served. The parent frequently needs to acquaint the palate of the young child with new, unfamiliar foods. This is important nutritionally as well as educationally. The child with limited selection of foods is a deprived child. This limits the scope of future life experiences such as dining with friends, visiting restaurants, and traveling to other countries. The child is required to eat a small amount of all foods. If the child refuses to eat a particular food, then he will not be allowed to eat anything else served with the particular refused food. Obviously no dessert will be served to the child. The next day he will be offered the same food until he eats the refused food. When the child realizes you are serious it will not take a long time for him to comply.

QUESTION: How can I stop my child from eating too much junk food?

SOLUTION: If the parent refuses to buy junk food it will not be in the house for the child to eat. There are many kinds of healthy foods that can be made available for snacking which are nutritionally good for the child. The parent should role model good eating habits.

QUESTION:  What can I do when my child does not eat the lunch I send with him to school?

SOLUTION:  The child and parent should discuss why the child is not eating the lunch.  If the problem is too much food, pack less.  If the problem is the kind of food, have the child help choose the foods for lunch limiting the choices to the proper nutrition requirements of children.  Learning about nutrition should be an ongoing process for the child so he sees the importance of eating well.  If the problem is trading food with friends be sure there are enough good foods for him to eat and something left to trade unless you forbid the child to trade food and require him to eat only his own lunch.

QUESTION:  How can I stop my child from using profanity?

SOLUTION:  Tell the child this is not an acceptable manner of speaking.  If the child says other children talk like this the parent responds, " It does not matter, it is wrong for you to talk like that." If the child says, "I heard you say that word" the parent response is, "I am an adult and can use adult language and you are a child and cannot use that language under any circumstances."  Parents need to set and enforce limits.

QUESTION:  How can I stop my child from bullying another child?

SOLUTION:  Bullying behavior has to be immediately addressed. Intimidating a weaker individual into doing things to profit oneself can be a highly addictive behavior.  The parent has to immediately let the child know that this kind of behavior is morally reprehensible (*See Chapter 5: Conscience Development & Creating Rational and Calibrated Guilt*).

The parent can use a "misdeed-pain association" by taking away a privilege or using corporal punishment to change this behavior. The important issue is that the child realizes abusing others will eventually end in bringing harm and disgrace to himself. A strong and secure person protects the fragile innocence of another while only a coward preys on the defenseless ones. The explanation to the bully should touch on the fact that often a less physically imposing individual who has the "power of right" emanating from within will embarrass the bully. Eventually, any bully will be exposed as a coward. The parents need to emphasize it is their love for the child that is motivating them to take a strong stance against his bullying behavior. The parents need to review the type and amount of loving their child is receiving since a bullying child is usually deficient in this area.

QUESTION: How can I make my child stop sleeping in my bed?

SOLUTION: A child should not have been encouraged or been allowed to begin sleeping in the parent's bed. An ill child's crib or bed can be temporarily put into the parent's bedroom for observation purposes until the child is feeling better, but the child still sleeps in her own bed. A child sleeping in the parent's bed may initially appear cute and cuddly, but will soon become a problem by frequently interrupting and limiting intimate physical contact as well as communication between spouses. A child cannot remain in the parent's bed. The child needs to be placed in his own bed. The longer he stays in the parent's bed, the more intense will be the child's resistance to being moved out into his own bed. A battle will ensue and the parent must win for the sake of the child's healthy development. *(See Chapter 3 for elements of winning battle and Chapter 5: Obedience Training.)*

Either parents or the single parent and surrogate parent need to agree upon the importance of the child sleeping in his own bed. Without a consensus, the battle should be postponed until unity is reached. Even with unity the battle will be arduous because changing this habit is not easy. The parent can spend time with the child in the child's room, reading a story, singing songs, saying prayers, but expect a strong negative reaction by the child when the parent leaves the room. The crying and screaming will decrease when the child realizes the parent's resolve. Depending on the age of the child, obedience training in other areas will lessen the process of developing proper sleeping habits.

QUESTION: My child is a "sore loser" and always has to be first. How can I change this attitude?

SOLUTION: The parent must understand that failure or losing is necessary for success. If we shy away from challenges to insure our illusion of perfection we will not be motivated to develop and grow. In essence, a parent has to teach the child the moral lesson that winning or losing is not easy to define. An individual may win a game that he put little effort into but has also lost because he developed a poor habit. On the other hand a particular game may have been lost by the team but won by the individual who put forth tremendous effort and raised his skill level making future wins a greater possibility.

When a child exhibits poor sportsmanship the best medicine is to increase the frequency of his losing. The parent should find opportunities to beat the child in checkers or at baseball or on a favorite video game and take the opportunity to give the child an understanding of progress rather than focusing on the outcome of the game. Letting the child win is not a good strategy. The child needs to know where he stands in his ability. If he wins fair and square it is a different story. He can then enjoy his victory. If the adult player lets the child win by not playing well, the child is not fine tuning his skills in order to become a better player, but is given a false sense of his ability to play the game.

QUESTION: What do I do when my child hugs and kisses me instead of doing what she is told?

SOLUTION: Do not be fooled by this behavior. This is a form of defiance. The child is manipulating the parent by the use of affection in this case to circumvent the command. The parent should stick to his guns and insist the child complete what was asked. The child may escalate the incident, but the parent needs to win this skirmish.

Remember when the child does what a parent requests consistently, a habit is formed which reduces the likelihood that disobedience will resurface for a reasonable request.

QUESTION: What should I do when my child throws a tantrum in a store?

SOLUTION: Immediately remove the child from the store. The shopping cart can wait. Go back to the car and tell the child that unless he stops acting like this you are going home without completing any shopping. That means no food, toys, or whatever. If the child does not calm down you have no choice but to leave the parking lot and return home. As soon as you have an adult who can stay with the child, go shopping without him. Before leaving you need to tell him why you cannot take him and that you will not buy anything for him because of the way he acted the last time you went shopping. After several trips without the child you may want to try taking him again but be prepared to leave if the behavior is not acceptable.

QUESTION: How do I stop my child from continually hitting his younger sibling?

SOLUTION: The rule should be established that no child should hit another family member. This rule should be religiously enforced to demonstrate the resolve of the parents. It may appear "cute" to some people for the younger child to hit the older one, but will usually lead to retaliation by the older child. Encouraging the children to share and play fairly will prevent many conflicts. When a conflict arises between siblings, they need to learn to communicate their difficulties with each other and if this fails, to a parent for resolution. The parents need to demonstrate good judgement whether to mete out consequences or not. When and if an older child abuses his power in dealing with a younger sibling, a dose of guilt should be administered for the poor leadership being shown as the older child (*See Chapter 5 Creating Rational and Calibrated Guilt for the Misdeed*).

QUESTION: What do I do when my child points to the desired object rather than saying the word? How can I make him say "please" and "thank you"?

SOLUTION: If a child has the ability to speak but does not name the object that is wanted, it would be irresponsible to give the child the object. Giving into the child by not demanding socially acceptable behavior will encourage lazy language and poor mannerly behavior development. Before giving the child anything, the child should be required to say "please" and the object's name and then say "thank you" after receiving it. If the child fails to follow this requirement the child should not receive anything. Only by using the right terms and proper niceties should they get the object in question. If "thank you" is forgotten the object should be taken back. Language and development of manners is a training issue falling primarily on the shoulders of the parents.

QUESTION: How do I change the attitude of a child who wants to receive money for anything he does?

SOLUTION: This means the child has been poorly trained in

understanding the reality of the family (*See Chapter 5: Reality Training*). If the child refuses to do something assigned by the parents, the parents should have a "sit down strike" to send a definite message to the child. The parent could stop driving the child to his activities, stop cooking, washing clothes, until the child realizes the importance of being a team member. The message is: "When everyone works together, everyone profits. When one member acts selfishly everyone suffers."

The concept of family teamwork is strengthened by the parent's effort connecting the efforts of the child with their effort. Whatever event or activity such as going to the beach, getting ice cream or a video that the family normally does should be pointed out as a benefit or reward for the work done by the family ( *This is a giving consequence discussed in Chapter 4.*)). The commonly held idea that children receive allowances for their work around the house may be sending the wrong message to some children. A child may think his parents should reward him or bribe him in order to motivate him to do the work he should be doing as part of the family. The ultimate reward for the child is being lucky enough to be a member of a functioning family.

QUESTION: How do I deal with my mother, who refuses to comply with the rules and standards my wife and I are attempting to instill in our children?

SOLUTION: Consistency in parental interaction with a child creates a healthy emotional and mental environment for the child. Different sets of rules and expectations place a child in unnecessary conflict and confusion. Ideally all significant adults involved in raising a child should be in agreement concerning their child rearing practices. Grandparents often have a different perspective because of age and responsibility and have a tendency to be more lenient and protective of their grandchildren. When the differences between the parent's and grandparent's perspective is slight, the benefits to the child being with a loving grandparent outweighs the disadvantages.

When there is open hostility and sabotage of the parents by the grandparents then the disadvantages may outweigh the advantages. The parents and grandparents should sit down and communicate like adults and come to agreement on negotiated guidelines. If this cannot be done without a third party then a mental health professional should be utilized. Working together is necessary for the sake of the child. If it is impossible to come to a reasonable agreement then the most responsible adults should prevail.

QUESTION: How does a parent know when a child's behavior is a problem or just normal developmental behavior?

SOLUTION: Any time your child's behavior is a concern, closely monitor the behavior. This way you can precisely describe the offensive behavior. You should ask yourself if the particular behavior is helpful, neutral or harmful to the envisioned future development of your child. Any uncertainty in answering this question can be resolved through discussions with respected adults including professionals. By getting other's ideas you can better formulate your own approach to this specific behavior by your child. Whether to ignore or confront your child's behavior will be determined by your ever evolving child rearing philosophy gained through your observation, intuition and knowledge learned from others.

QUESTION: How can parents deal with feeling sorry for their child because he was ill or because of a death in the family?

SOLUTION: Many parents have a tendency to allow their child's behavior to slide for awhile after a tragedy. The rationale is that the child has suffered enough already and they do not want to add to the child's burden. The problem with this strategy is two-fold.

First, the child develops bad habits, which need to be corrected taking time and energy away from more pleasurable pursuits. Second, death and illness are ongoing issues. Parents have to help the child prepare by teaching her how to cope with the event and place it in a bigger context gaining an understanding of life and death.

The younger the child the more simplistic the parental message to the child. The child will feed off the emotional response of the parent. If the parent is calm and speaks of a loved one going to heaven then the message is clear and persuasive. Answering the child's direct questions on these issues is much more effective than to ignore the incident in helping guide the child through the tough times in life.

QUESTION: What can I do when the school says my child needs to be put on psychotropic drugs such as Ritalin or Prozac?

SOLUTION: Immediately request a conference with the appropriate school personnel. Obtain from them the reasons for their difficulty with your child. Inform them you will seek out a mental health professional and nutritionist to help you develop a behavioral and nutritional program to get the child back on the right track. Find a professional who has success with non-compliant children. Read materials like this book that will help you regain power in your relationship with your child.

Work closely with school personnel to demonstrate improvement at home and obtain feedback on how the child is doing in school. Tell the school you are willing to continue to work with the mental health, nutrition professionals and your child to insure his improvement at school. For any continuing problem that arises at school you will be supportive of the school personnel and the school's intervention. You will also give your child consequences at home for misdeeds at school.

By working closely with the school instead of against them you will probably be allowed time to help your child develop more appropriate school behaviors without the need for medication.

QUESTION: What do I do with an ADHD child who has inappropriate, impulsive behavior?

SOLUTION: The label ADHD does not exonerate a child's misdeeds anymore than an "insanity plea" exonerates a murderer. Any individual, young or old, needs to receive a reasonable consequence for destructive acts in order to assist the person in developing inhibiting behavior to counter their impulsive tendencies (*See Chapter 3:and Chapter 5: The Wrap*). Making excuses for or ignoring a child's inappropriate actions is a guaranteed method of producing an inattentive and irresponsible child without limits to their behavior. A child needs to be held accountable for his actions to gain the knowledge that his choices will result in positive or negative reactions. Placing the ADD or ADHD label or administering drugs to the child does not relieve the parent of the need to continue to teach the child to listen and accept the reasonable consequences for their good or bad choices and resulting behavior.

QUESTION: What do I do with a child five years old who pretends to play for several hours a day with an imaginary friend?

SOLUTION: A child who creates an imaginary playmate has insufficient connection with other people. The child with a pretend friend has too much time spent alone. The parent prepares the environment with siblings or peers to help the child learn interactional skills and getting along with others. A pet without the ability for verbal communication can teach the child about the world outside of oneself. The cat purring, the dog running in a circle, the fish swimming concretely demonstrate reality to the child.

It is the job of the parents to place their child in experiences that will help the child succeed in life. Story reading, trips to the store, visits to friends or relations, discussing the child's day are constantly strung together to create a healthy growth environment for a child. Many confused parents view an imaginary playmate as cute, creative, and as a harmless way to occupy the child while they are busy in their harried life style. Their child's need to pretend to have a friend should be a red flag that warns the parent their child is starving for real interaction with others, especially the parents. Parents need to provide children opportunities to create imtimacy.

QUESTION: What should I do when my six-year-old child is questioning the existence of Santa Claus?

SOLUTION: It is best for the parent to be truthful with their child. A parent can explain the spirit of Christmas is a positive force and is real in the minds of individuals. By relating that Santa Claus is a symbol of that spirit, before the child's peers ridicule him for believing in Santa, the parents retain their credibility with their children. When a child has faith in the words of his parents, the child will be more likely to be open with them concerning personal issues.

QUESTION: How do I stop my child from calling other adults and me by our first names?

SOLUTION: The child should use the names "mother" and "father" or their derivatives instead of first names. The words "father" and "mother" are inherently terms of respect. To encourage or allow the use of first names by a child places everyone on an equal footing. This may make a parent or adult feel younger, like a child, but obliterates the distinctions between child and adult and gives the child a distorted picture of reality (*See Chapter 5, Reality Training*).

QUESTION: What happens when a parent evaluates and elevates their child above others at all times (plays favorites)?

SOLUTION: This is a perfect prescription to set ones child up for failure. A child in the short term will be happy with his parent's positive appraisal of his performance. However, in the long run when other authority figures give a more honest though lower evaluation, his parents may be resented for not preparing him for reality. Doing a quality job cannot be accomplished by cheerleading, pretending, or wishful thinking. Instead, it takes consistent effort.

A child needs to be told how to improve her performance not be told everything she does is terrific. A good coach points out the deficiencies in a player's game and then demonstrates the right way to do the play. The psychological establishment's almost religious belief in positive reinforcement has been demonstrated to elevate self-esteem without a positively correlating effect on performance.

Parents believe through positive reinforcement their child will be emotionally healthy and also love them. In reality, this strategy develops a child who expects praise even when his effort and quality of work is poor. In loving their children parents need to be honest in the appraisal of their abilities and shortcomings to challenge the child to reach higher levels of performance.

QUESTION: Most experts say that corporal punishment will foster a violent child, so what should a parent do about spanking?

SOLUTION: Spanking a young child, one to ten years old, on the behind is a time tested method of getting the child's immediate attention. Once the child halts his negative behavior usually by crying, the parent needs to ask why he received a spanking. The child should exhibit remorse and take responsibility for his *misbehavior (See Chapter 5: The Wrap & Conscience Development).* If the child acts like he does not understand why he was physically reprimanded, the parent should precisely state what the child did wrong. The child needs to say what the parent said displaying awareness and responsibility for his action. Corporal punishment has been used since antiquity and is a humane act, not an abusive act when used to train a child to behave in a socially appropriate way. Hitting a child is abusive, however, and will teach violence when the physical confrontation is to relieve the emotional anger of the parent and is not part of a training program.

Each solution to a specific question or FAQ should not be viewed in isolation from the principles and philosophical rationale that support the systematic Essential Parenting™ presented in this book.

Essential Parenting™ starts by establishing the concrete love of meeting survival needs and sequentially proceeds to the more and more complex and abstract forms of love, which culminate with the child becoming an independent adult. This adult returns that love to his own children, family, community and nation. Essential Parenting™ is anchored in Judeo-Christian values that reestablish the family as the most important social unit in our nation and the parents as the head of the family, responsible for training the children to be respectful, moral, contributing members of society. Through the implementing of Essential Parenting™ modern confused parents can save their children from a life of self-centered, immoral materialism and place them upon the road that will produce a more responsible, empathetic, and appreciative individual. This truly is the ultimate legacy for one's life.

# *Afterward: The Cultural Civil War*

There would be no need for <u>ESSENTIAL PARENTING</u>™:
<u>*Revitalizing and Re-moralizing the Family in the 21^(st) Century*</u>, if
our society was in balance. In the beginning of the 21^(st) century
our nation is so dramatically leaning to the side of individual
expression without personal responsibility and away from family
and community responsibilities that there has been a serious
weakening of society. If all behaviors are tolerated and treated
equally, civilization, as we understand it, will cease to exist. If a
nation no longer clearly defines ideals of morality, manners,
ethics, and beliefs for it's children, but instead offers a mind
boggling array of choices of behavior with an "anything goes"
attitude then confusion, insecurity, and eventual anarchy will
follow. By society placing sociopathic behavior on an equal par
with law-abiding behavior; immorality with morality; homosexual
behavior with heterosexual behavior; and narcissistic behavior
with serving family, community, and God; the necessary
distinctions which define the culture and which a nation expects
it's citizens to exhibit, are eliminated.

A society which selectively uses national opinion polls of the
general population instead of ancestral wisdom passed down by

the brightest and wisest citizens is creating a society based on political expediency not principles and truth. National leaders, politicians, educators, business people, or clergy who pander to the self-indulgence of the masses rather than inspire to greater truth are laying the foundation for a society which regresses into pockets of exploitive self-interest. A society led by national leaders with weak or non-existent principles will use censorship of the media to keep citizens ignorant of the abuses of their power. It often appears that the national television networks, major newspapers, and cable news providers collaborate with the Federal government to not print all the truth, but only to print what will advance the government's position.

In this environment, parents need to educate and protect their children from governmental assaults on the values the parents hold sacred. Parents need to protect against homosexual marriages, homosexuals as Boy Scout leaders, and the National Man-Boy Love Association, which are threats to the healthy development of the sexual orientation of young children and the welfare of the family while doing nothing to promote or benefit the propagation of our species or to replenish our population. Therefore, society should have little motivation to promote deviant sexual behavior, but ought to have great motivation to shun this alternative lifestyle as it competes with and undermines the backbone of a healthy society: the family.

It takes great leaders and role models who have character, wisdom, and strong principles to instill positive spirit into a nation for individuals to rise above their base instincts. In the same manner, it takes dedicated parents with character, wisdom, and principles to teach and train their children to be good family members and citizens of a community. Our great historical leaders, George Washington, Abraham Lincoln, and Theodore Roosevelt did not do what was popular by taking polls, but led the nation through difficult times guided by their traditional value system. Great leaders inspire others to do things beyond their normal vision. Positive family role models: fathers, mothers, sisters, brothers have the same power to inspire family and community members to look for serving God through others while negative role models have the power to lower expectations and values to vulgar self-interest and exploitative levels.

Without parents giving more than material things to their children, each succeeding generation will be less able and equipped to manage the complexities of modern life. The family unit is the fulcrum of a healthy and vibrant society, not individuals nor the state. When self-interest reigns, society has chaos. When the state reigns we have totalitarianism. When the family is nourished and strong, society is in the natural balance between the forces of the self-interest of the individual, community and nation.

ESSENTIAL PARENTING™: Revitalizing and Re-moralizing the Family in the 21st Century is the social remedy to restore that balance. Essential Parenting™ helps the parent to gain or regain control of their family. Once the parents are in charge they are able to inculcate traditional morals and values to their children. As parents learn and practice Essential Parenting™ the child will have greater stability, self-discipline, and mental health while parents will have a greater sense of purpose, confidence, and fulfillment as parents. Through the process of Purposeful Discipline parents are able to teach and train their children to be civilized and competent members of a healthy society. When many families practice Essential Parenting™ then we will turn the cultural tide.

Thank you for reading <u>Essential Parenting</u>™. We hope through the energetic implementation of the concepts and strategies outlined in this book your children and eventually society will reap the desired benefits.

Sincerely,

Domenick and Julie Maglio